To the Ends of the Earth

VISIONS OF A CHANGING WORLD: 175 YEARS OF EXPLORATION AND PHOTOGRAPHY

To the Ends of the Earth

VISIONS OF A CHANGING WORLD: 175 YEARS OF EXPLORATION AND PHOTOGRAPHY

BLOOMSBURY

First published in Great Britain 2005
Bloomsbury Publishing Plc, 38 Soho Square, London W1D 3HB

A CIP catalogue record for this book is available from the British Library

Published by arrangement with Book Creation Ltd., London,
and Book Creation LLC, New York
Publishing Directors: Hal Robinson and John Kelly

Photography permissions:

© Photographs reproduced under licence from the Royal Geographical Society, London, unless otherwise stated in the picture acknowledgements on page 240. All maps in the publications are used for illustrative purposes only. All rights reserved.

Rolex supports the Society's collection of maps, photographs, books and documents. Recently Rolex has supported the photographic library, including the Everest archive that illustrates the British climbs from 1921 to the successful ascent in 1953.

Contributors:
Dr Rita Gardner, Professor Robin Butlin, Jonathan Bastable and Steve Brace.

Special thanks to Pauline Hubner, Justin Hobson and Francis Herbert at the Royal Geographical Society (with IBG) for all their help and advice in the preparation of this book.

The editors gratefully acknowledge the invaluable contribution made by Professor Robin Butlin to the overall conception and development of this book.

Managing Editor: David Popey
Art Editor: Keith Miller
Design consultant: Peter Laws
Copy Editors: Zoë Ross, Ali Moore and Tami Rex
Proofreading: Kim Davies and Jane Egginton

Photographs on pages:
2. Shekhawati children, India. Photo: Chris Caldicott
3. Bactrian camels crossing the sand dunes at Tsagaan Nuur, Mongolia. Photo: RGS
5. The Oman Wahiba Sands Project 1985–1987. Photo: Michael Keating
6. Kaieteur Falls, Potaro River, Guyana in 1878 by Everard Im Thurn. Photo: RGS

Front cover: A view of Ellsworth Mountains, Antarctica. Photo: Bruce Herrod
Back cover: The 'Pilgrim's Rest', Burma. Photo: RGS
Jacket flap (back): A mosque constructed from mud at Diafarabe, Mali. Photo: Chris Caldicott
Jacket flap (front): Gauthgame Point, west coast of Australia (top). Photo: Joann Crowther;
Herbert Ponting's view of the Great Wall of China, 1907 (bottom). Photo: RGS.
Spine photograph: The summit of a sand hill, Saudi Arabia by Harry St John Philby. Photo: RGS

Printed and bound in China

ISBN 0-7475-8138 X

10 9 8 7 6 5 4 3 2 1

CONTENTS

FOREWORD

One hundred and seventy-five years ago the Royal Geographical Society was established to promote "the advancement of geographical science".

Today, we can look back with some satisfaction and pride on the work of the Society, which took people to the limits of their known world and beyond. And perhaps few other bodies have had such influence on how contemporary culture sees today's world. Generations owe their knowledge and understanding of the world's people, places and environment to the information captured in the detailed maps, stunning photographs and compelling writing of those who have contributed to the Society: Dr. David Livingstone, Freya Stark, Captain Scott, Sir Ernest Shackleton, Sir Edmund Hillary and Tenzing Norgay are just some of the outstanding people to whom all of us should be grateful.

It is this distinguished history, and the knowledge and experience that go with it, that informs our endeavours today. In a world of ever-increasing complexity, the need to understand has never been greater. It is here that the Society's work in educating future generations, supporting academic research and field science, and opening up its unique collections to the public are of such importance.

There are no longer any blanks on the world map. But the blanks of ignorance and misunderstanding make the task of the Society more important than it has ever been—for all those whose interest, travel, work or imagination take them to the ends of the earth.

Sir Neil Cossons OBE, President, Royal Geographical Society (with IBG)

RECENT DEVELOPMENTS AND FUTURE PROSPECTS

Rita Gardner, Director, Royal Geographical Society

The new entrance to the Royal Geographical Society on Exhibition Road features a glass balustrade created by Eleanor Long.
Photo: James Morris

VISIONS OF A CHANGING WORLD

This book is a celebration of the opening of the Society's great collections to the public in 2004. The collections are there for everyone who wishes to access the endeavours, the knowledge and the extraordinary changes in our world and its peoples that they record. They tell of adventure and heroism, discovery and understanding, culture and environment as seen through the eyes of western explorers, scholars, travellers, diplomats and colonial administrators. It is inevitably a partial view.

In the following chapters we see the collections linked back to their roots in the Society's remarkable history and to a selection of the many extraordinary people who led the search for "new" knowledge, often in inhospitable areas. The concept of geographical exploration and scientific research has changed much over that time. The early mapping and description of features, places and indigenous peoples have given way to investigations of the causes and processes that bring about changes in environments, societies and cultures, both locally and globally, and the interconnections between them. Exploration has evolved into scientific research on the one hand and, on the other, into a personal search for new experiences and physical achievement.

The Society's overall purpose has changed relatively little in 175 years; it is still "advancing geographical science". The search for new knowledge and understanding remains a driving force, as does the desire to use its knowledge, standing and influence to advance education. But its ethos, how it achieves these ends, its status as a professional body as well as a learned society, and the scale and breadth of audiences that it reaches out to, are very different, and refreshingly so. Many of its Fellows and Members remain as passionate about travel as ever, and with the Society having charitable status since the 1960s, it now exists to serve, first and foremost, the public benefit.

THE SOCIETY IN 2005

The Royal Geographical Society (with the Institute of British Geographers) reaches 175 years of age with much to celebrate. A period of growth over the past 25 years, culminating in the strategic changes and developments of the past seven years, has transformed it into a leading learned society and professional body for the new millennium. It currently has 14,000 members and nine regional branches, and it reaches out to hundreds of thousands of people each year, nationally and internationally. It is the largest and most active scholarly geographical society in the world.

Responding to technological changes, and to issues of access and relevance, the Society has expanded its activities and created a balanced portfolio supporting geographical research, education, expeditions and fieldwork, public engagement, policy and its membership. It has achieved this without core government funding, and while simultaneously developing its breadth of activities and refurbishing and extending its facilities. A new visual identity was introduced in 2004 to coincide with the public opening of the collections and the launch of the new buildings and facilities. This was preceded in 2003 by the introduction of a readily accessible form of membership, which is open to all, to sit alongside Fellowship.

The Society has evolved, carrying its supporters with it and building on its strengths and traditions. The recent changes have established a strong foundation for future developments in support of that "most relevant of disciplines—geography". In summer 2005, the Society published its second strategy, having achieved most of what it set out to do in its first one.

THE IMPETUS FOR CHANGE

The recent history of the Royal Geographical Society (with the Institute of British Geographers) is both a story of continuing evolution, and a story of rapid and lasting change. It has undoubtedly been one of the greatest periods of development in the Society's 175 years.

The primary impetus came in 1995 with the merger between the Royal Geographical Society and the Institute of British Geographers. The success of the negotiations reflected the commitment of honorary officers from both bodies, and was in no small part due to the highly experienced chairmanship of the merger working group by Sir Crispin Tickell, then President of the Royal Geographical Society.

Historically the Royal Geographical Society had spawned new geographical bodies, notably the Geographical Association and the Institute of British Geographers, partly because the Society either could not or chose not to meet the emerging needs of the geographical community at the time. In 1995, for the first time, the Society was faced with an entirely new experience—a genuine merger between two authoritative and prestigious subject bodies.

Each organization had its individual, and largely different identities and constituencies. The two organizations delivered highly complementary activities in support of geography nationally and internationally, albeit with some notable gaps and inequalities. The memberships of both had concerns about "take-over", probably in equal measure, as well as differing expectations of future development and change.

CREATING A NEW VISION

For the first year the two bodies were effectively "bolted together", with the former Institute of British Geographers' activities being incorporated into a new Research and Higher Education Department in the RGS-IBG, and with changes to the governance to reflect and safeguard the different constituencies.

Retaining support and all the core activities of both organizations, while forging an identifiably new and single body in the eyes of the membership, the staff and the outside world was a much longer process, at the heart of which was the formulation of the Society's first strategic plan. After an extensive phase of consultation throughout 1997, this was published in early 1998. The plan built on the dual traditions and strengths of the merged organizations, while embracing the need for change: evolution, not revolution, was the aim of this process.

The plan set out the vision for a more outward-looking and inclusive organization, and firmly established the concept of balance across the Society's different areas of activity, embodied in six objectives. These centred on supporting and promoting geographical research and education (including expedition and fieldwork-related activities); the provision of information; public understanding; policy-related activities; and the continuing vigour of the Society and its Fellowship.

The Society's mission was articulated as: "A world centre for geographers and geographical learning dedicated to the development and promotion of knowledge together with its application to the challenges facing society and the environment." This provided a guiding interpretation of the Society's objective of "advancing geographical science" as set out in the Royal Charter of 1859.

A MATTER OF IMAGE

Perceptions of the Society differed greatly in 1995. For some, an old-school atmosphere was highly valued; for others the Society was perceived less positively as an exclusive élite, despite the fact that many of its activities were open to all and had been for many years. The challenge was to be, and to be seen to be, open and inclusive, while retaining the independence and standing of the organization, its brand and its distinctive character.

That vision has been realized in a number of ways, and the Society has been opened up—intellectually, visually and physically. The most visually obvious change was the creation of contemporary new buildings in June 2004. This placed the Society's front door directly on Exhibition Road—visited by more than nine million people a year—and created an open, accessible and welcoming new entrance and display space as a "shop window" for geography in one of the greatest learning and cultural quarters in the world. The combination of modern new spaces and refurbished older traditional ones, sitting comfortably alongside one another, symbolizes the approach that has typified the Society's recent developments. That is, an ability to build on tradition, while welcoming the new, and demonstrating the modern relevance of the organization and the discipline of geography.

The new spaces were warmly received by the architectural press, and the "thinking architecture" of the new buildings not only delivered the modern feel and function that was sought, but also made the most of a tight urban site, and opened new vistas of London's heritage. The development was part of the largest combined building and refurbishment programme in the Society's history. It also included the splendid and complete refurbishment of the historic Ondaatje Theatre, first built in 1930 as part of the Society's centenary celebrations, and the creation of a 100-seat education centre and a seminar suite on the ground floor of Lowther Lodge. The superb facilities help to facilitate the archives' access project and much more.

MAKING THE MOST OF OUR RESOURCES

The location of the Society is but one of its key strengths. The others are the knowledge and expertise of Fellows, other members and staff; and the scope, depth and diversity of the collections. All have been engaged to great effect and to varying degrees in the recent developments.

Most of the new building was created as part of the £7.2 million project to "unlock" the Society's archives. Supported financially by the Heritage Lottery Fund and many other Trusts and Foundations as well as by donations from Fellows, this project has provided public access for the first time to the remarkable collections of more than two million items, including more than 500,000 heritage items pre-dating 1920.

Access takes various forms, ranging from the ability to search the catalogues online to using the new Foyle Reading Room, a beautiful study space overlooking the newly landscaped garden. Added educational value of the heritage materials is provided through interpretation: the online learning resources for teachers and pupils, and onsite class visits. For the lifelong learner, there are exhibitions both in the new display space and online.

The Society's membership contributes its expertise in many ways: to the annual programme of 150 lectures and conferences in London and the nine regional branches, to committee deliberations, and to the new learning resources that aim to enhance geography teaching in schools. In the past five years, building on a long tradition of conferences for teachers, the Society has established an education department that supplies the teaching community with digital learning resources, continuing professional development courses, tools for "marketing" geography, careers information, and general advice and guidance.

The Society's expertise is also vital in the support of expeditions and fieldwork; the Expedition Advisory Centre continues to respond to 15,000 enquiries a year and has expanded its training courses. A particular new focus has been training for teachers, youth workers and expedition leaders in health, safety and risk management for fieldwork and expeditions.

WIDENING ACCESS: REACHING NEW AUDIENCES

A combination of technological changes, new ideas and new facilities has enabled the Society to reach out more effectively both to its existing audiences and to new ones.

In an innovative project in 1997, the Society was one of the first learned bodies to provide free access to an archive of one of its scholarly journals on the internet. This has since been developed, through partnerships with publishing agencies, to widen access further and subscribers can now find current and back issues of all three scholarly journals online. These constitute one of the world's leading sets of international geographical journals, and they have been augmented by a new Book Series.

The new facilities have also enabled the Society to hold its annual international conference at its own premises in London. With more than 1,000 attendees in recent years, it is the second largest annual conference of academic geographers in the world, It draws heavily on the expertise in the Society's 25 specialist research groups. In a departure from the norm, the Society's growing expertise in major conference organization also led to the invitation to coordinate the International Geographical Union Congress meeting in Glasgow in 2004, working alongside representatives from other UK geographical bodies in the organizing committee.

The development of new audiences is a key theme in opening the collections, especially in using the rich and culturally important map and photographic materials. The Society is currently evolving new partnerships with black and minority ethnic communities, and is actively involved in new audience development pilot projects.

Equally as important in terms of widening access was the vote by the membership in 2003 to introduce a new category of member, that of Ordinary Member, to complement the category of Fellow. Designed for those with a more general interest in geography and travel, it has proved to be popular and it helped to raise the membership level to more than 14,000 in 2004. Fellows and Members continue to be highly valued for their expertise, financial support and other assistance, but as a charity the Society serves first and foremost the public benefit.

WORKING WITH GOVERNMENT

The Society has developed its role in working with and for the geographical community in advocating changes in policy as it affects geographical education, research and fieldwork. The Policy and Public Affairs Unit was created in 2001 to assist in this process. Its work with government has also increased, both in terms of funded projects to support teaching and

The glass window and roof of the spiral staircase at the new extension at the Royal Geographical Society emphasise the constructive fusion between the Society's buildings, new and old.
Photos: James Morris

learning in schools and colleges, as well as raising the profile of geographical research in relevant policy areas through the media and conferences.

Among its advocacy successes, often achieved by working in partnership with others, are the revision of the teaching funding for geography in higher education; the establishment of Humanities Specialist Schools within the Specialist Schools Programme; the establishment and coordination of the Secretary of State for Education "Strategy Group for Geography"; and the provision of advice on health and safety in fieldwork.

FUNDRAISING

To support the new developments, so that they are not a strain on its traditional activities, the Society has both increased its core income and developed its fundraising capacity. Core income has expanded from the highly valued support of the membership and the corporate benefactors, and from enterprise activities.

Fundraising, which has been superbly supported by the fundraising advisory group led by the Earl of Selborne and a newly established Development Office, succeeded in raising the £11 million target for the Capital Appeal between 2000 and 2004. This included support for enhanced grant-giving for research, as well as for capital developments and website developments. A most generous gift from Sir Christopher Ondaatje launched the Appeal. In addition to the Capital Appeal, the Society has successfully raised project-based funding and maintained a supporting group of corporate partners.

In recent years its capacity for grant-giving to support research, expeditions and teaching has risen from £96,000 in 1998 to over £150,000 in 2004. The scope has also been widened to include more individual research grants and grants for postgraduates, as a complement to the traditional expedition team grants.

FUTURE PROSPECTS

Following the impetus for change that came from the merger with the Institute of British Geographers, combined with technological changes and a new political context, the Society has established itself as a single strong, dynamic and balanced institution. It is now one of the leading learned societies in the UK, and probably the largest and most active scholarly geographical society in the world. It has retained the support of the vast majority of its members throughout the development process, as well as gaining many new ones. It started 2005 with a strong platform of facilities, membership, external support, outreach work and activities on which to build future growth and development. Its new strategy, covering the period from 2005 to 2010, set out the Society's aspirations for this development.

For the first year at least the emphasis was on consolidation after a period of substantial evolution. Thereafter the aspiration continues to be to keep the support of geographical research and education (including expeditions and fieldwork) at the core of the Society. The strategy places increased emphasis on the Society's role in promoting public understanding and enhancing enjoyment of geography and the public image of the discipline, as well as on the Society's role in influencing policy debates with geographical perspectives. Core to this process are the roles of membership, staff and finance in underpinning all the activities in London, in the UK, and internationally.

The continually evolving wider context will undoubtedly deliver some unexpected challenges, but there will be new opportunities too, including UK, European-wide and international ones. One interesting opportunity is the proposed development of Exhibition Road, on which the Society is located, to create a cultural and learning "quarter" appropriate to the status of the Society and the 16 other world-class organizations based in the area. It may serve to re-ignite Prince Albert's original vision for the area as a public meeting place for the arts and sciences, and if so, the Society is ready to secure the place of geography within the modernized vision.

Luxor, as seen from a felucca, a lateen-rigged sailing vessel so characteristic of traditional sailing boats on the Nile.

CHAPTER 1
CHANGING VISIONS:
THE RGS IN THE 19TH CENTURY

CHANGING VISIONS: THE RGS IN THE 19TH CENTURY

Robin Butlin

Previous page: Mount Everest and the Himalayan range as pictured in the 1890s. Held in the RGS archives, it is thought to be one of the earliest images of the range ever taken.

Part of a map of RGS Fellows' addresses in London, marked by John Shillington, the RGS librarian, in 1843 on an 1842 Post Office Directory map of London.

The Geographical Society of London was founded in London in 1830. Under its first patron, King William IV, it was known as the Royal Geographical Society, and it received its Royal Charter (under Queen Victoria) in 1859. Before 1830, geographical issues had been debated at intellectual and social salons, including lively dining clubs in London. The Geographical Society was not even the first such association of its kind. Almost 50 years before, in 1788, the African Association (known more cumbersomely in full as The Association for Promoting the Interior Parts of Africa) was founded in a tavern off Pall Mall in central London. Its original 12 members all belonged to a dining club called the Saturday's Club, and the minutes of their first meeting have that purposeful air, a sense of setting the world to rights, that only descends after a really good dinner.

"No species of information," resolved the gentlemen, "is more ardently desired, or more generally useful, than that which improves the science of Geography; and as the vast continent of Africa, notwithstanding the efforts of the ancients, and the wishes of the moderns, is still in a great measure unexplored, the members of this club do form themselves into an Association for promoting the discovery of the inland parts of that quarter of the world."[1]

The founder members were all distinguished men, but the only genuine explorer among them was Sir Joseph Banks, President of the Royal Society. He was a naturalist and anthropologist who had travelled with James Cook on his first voyage of 1768. Other notable members included Lord Rawdon, Governor-General of India; Mr. Henry Beaufroy, a Quaker and Member of Parliament; and Sir John Sinclair, a Scottish landowner known for his interest in rural economy and economic statistics.

The common interests and qualities of all these men included considerable political experience, liberal views (including support for the abolition of the slave trade), a substantial knowledge of science (six were Fellows of the Royal Society), and an interest in Africa, then conceived as an almost empty space. The African Association was one of a string of new organizations whose purpose was the scientific investigation of little-known lands. These included the Linnaean Society (1788), the Palestine Association (1804), the Syrian Society (1805) and the Zoological Society (1826). Geographical societies were also established in Paris in 1822 and in Berlin in 1828.[2]

But the immediate antecedent of the Royal Geographical Society was the Raleigh Club, an informal group of "hardy and experienced explorers". This was another dining club, founded at the Thatched House restaurant in St James's Street in London in 1827. The principal mover of the Raleigh Club was Arthur de Capel Brooke, an army officer who had a special interest in travel in Scandinavia. His club rules stated that the members should,

through their travel experience, represent one or more parts of the world, so that between them, as far as possible, the globe as a whole would be covered.

On May 24, 1830, John Barrow, Second Secretary to the Admiralty, made the proposal that: "Among the numerous literary and scientific societies established in the British metropolis, one was still wanting to complete the circle of scientific institutions, whose sole object should be the promotion and diffusion of that most important and entertaining branch of knowledge, geography."[3]

His suggestion was that: "A new and useful Society might therefore be formed, under the name of The Geographical Society of London; that the interest excited by this department of science is universally felt; that its advantages are of the first importance to mankind in general, and paramount to the welfare of a maritime nation like Great Britain with its numerous and extensive foreign possessions."

The objectives of the proposed Society included the gathering and publication of new geographical information; the stocking of a geographical library with reference materials, including books, maps and charts; the obtaining and provision of appropriate instruments for survey and navigation; the provision of instructions, advice, guidance and a measure of selective financial support for travellers; and the exchange of information and publications with other geographical, philosophical and literary societies.

From the start the Society had close links with the political and scientific élite as well as the armed forces. Early documentation has shown that among the 460 members in 1830 there were three dukes, nine earls, 24 other peers, 24 baronets and knights, 32 naval officers and 55 army officers. Of these, 124 were Fellows of the Royal Society.[4] The first decades of the Society were overseen by a succession of presidents who were prominent members of the establishment: aristocrats, senior army and navy officers, diplomats, lawyers and colonial administrators. But two stand out above the rest: John Barrow, the Raleigh Club member who drafted the Society's original aims and principles; and Roderick Murchison, a soldier-scientist who did pioneering work on the geological timescale. Barrow was President from 1835–37, and Murchison was four times President, in 1843–45, 1851–53, 1856–59 and 1862–71.

BARROW AND MURCHISON—THE PIONEERS

John Barrow (1764–1848) was an archetypal explorer and a tough man. As a young man Barrow sailed to the Arctic on a whaler, then returned to teach mathematics in a school in Greenwich, London. He also worked in China for two years, visited South Africa in 1792, served the governor of Cape Colony, then committed himself to government work at the Admiralty. He was elected a Fellow of the Royal Society in 1805, and as vice-president promoted exploration of the Arctic and Australia. He wrote many books about his experiences of travel in eastern Asia and southern Africa, as well as several biographies and a large number of articles for scholarly reviews. His energy and determination made him a key figure in the advancement of the Society, and of geography more generally.

Roderick Murchison (above, left) was a powerful supporter of David Livingstone's African expeditions. The explorer dedicated his best-selling book to him. John Barrow (below) was a founder member and the third president of the RGS. A strait and a point in the Arctic are named after him, as is a species of duck—the Barrow Goldeye.

But it is Barrow's contemporary, Roderick Murchison (1792–1871), who bestrides the first half-century of the Society like a colossus. He was born in the Highlands, and was blessed with a gift for scientific exploration. He spent the early part of his adult life as a soldier, before turning to the study of geology and carrying out an extensive survey of the Russian Empire. He became a Fellow of the Geological Society in 1825 and its president in 1831.

Bottom: 15 Whitehall Place, where the RGS had a base in rented rooms from 1854 to 1870, and below, its home from 1871 at 1 Saville Row, "the Mecca of all true geographers".

Murchison's influence on geological and geographical knowledge was immense. He was also a fine publicist, and used this skill to promote the Society. His biographer, R. A. Stafford, has said that "his sophisticated manipulation of publicity techniques transformed the ailing Society into a theatre of national suspense, a company of talented adventurers purveying high drama in exotic settings with himself as manager/director. Just as Murchison himself had thrilled to the challenge of 'geologizing' the wilds of Russia, Britons bored by their tame landscape found excitement in vicariously following the explorers on pilgrimages to distant and savage lands. The exploits of these geographical heroes were symbolic as well as real, for they demonstrated the fitness of the nation for dominion over palm, pine and native races."[5]

It was Murchison who, in 1871, arranged the purchase of 1 Savile Row as a permanent headquarters for the Society. Before this, meetings had been held at various locations around London: the Horticultural Society in Regent Street; a rented house in Waterloo Place; and a building on Whitehall Place that was adapted at some expense to accommodate the Society's requirement for offices, a map and chart room, library, council chamber and a small lecture theatre. The lecture theatre in the new four-storey building on the corner of a fashionable street was much larger, and the new headquarters even boasted an observatory on the roof.

Before long the very address was so closely associated with adventure that it thrilled the heart of explorers everywhere. The Society's historian H. R. Mill has written that "for more than forty years 1 Savile Row was the Mecca of all true geographers, the home port of every traveller … The earlier homes of the Society have been swallowed up in the

transformation of London, but even when 1 Savile Row also passes away the spirit of geography must surely continue to haunt that corner."[6]

That "spirit of geography" was laid down over the decades like a rich patina on a polished map table. The Society's influence proceeded not just from the lectures and dinners held at Savile Row, or from the books written or researched in its library. The officers and council of the Society made their presence felt by engaging in public debate and expressing their views in the letters column of *The Times* and other newspapers. Crucially, they maintained close contact with departments of state, including the Admiralty, the Colonial Office, the India Office, the War Office and the Foreign Office.[7]

Partly as a result of these semi-official links with government, the Society became closely involved with the geopolitical problems facing Britain in the middle of the 19th century. Chief among these troubles was Russia's expansion into Central Asia, a development that was seen to

Thomas Baines' lush watercolour of the Victoria Falls, made in 1862. Baines's works were the first images ever to be made of the Falls. The spear-throwing African man in the corner adds a special touch of drama, and is designed to appeal to a Victorian viewing public.

be a major threat to British India. Russian armies had been edging southeast through Turcoman territory since the beginning of the 1830s, annexing one city after another and forcing their khans to submit to the tsar's authority. Tashkent fell to the Russians in 1865, Samarkand and Bokhara in 1868 and Khiva—the perfect staging post for a march on India—in 1873. Meanwhile British forces were progressing northward through the sub-continent, taking Sind in 1843, Kashmir in 1846, the Punjab in 1849 and Baluchistan in 1859.[8] The two superpowers seemed to be on a collision course.

THE FORCE OF GEOPOLITICS

There were different responses from Britain to this perceived threat. The so-called "Forward School" held the view that Britain needed to block the Russian menace by creating a buffer state in Afghanistan. The main proponent of this idea was Henry Rawlinson, a Fellow of the Society. He had worked for the East India Company in India and had served as an MP. In 1865 Rawlinson published an article in the *Quarterly Review*, noting the northward advance of British India and the southward advance of Russia. He deplored what he saw as the indifference of the British public to the Russian threat.

In the very year that the Russians took Khiva he became President of the RGS. In this influential post he continued to comment on the diplomacy and military geostrategy in the region, which had already been dubbed "the Great Game".

In 1875 Rawlinson published a book entitled *England and Russia in the East; a Series of Papers on the Political and Geographical Condition of Central Asia*. Its opinion on the politics of the region was shared by Disraeli's government, which took office in 1874. An army was sent from India to take Afghanistan and so set a limit—an uncrossable line—to Russian advancement. But when Gladstone became prime minister in 1879, he recalled the army while it was on its way to Kabul.

Sir Rutherford Alcock, President of the RGS from 1876–78. In 1844 he was appointed consul at Fuchow in China, where, after a short official stay at Amoy, he performed the functions "of everything from a lord chancellor to a sheriff's officer".

The Society continued to influence British foreign policy all the same. In March 1882 a lecture at the Royal Geographical Society by Edmund O'Donovan, a *Daily News* correspondent, prompted further discussion by Rawlinson and others of the danger from Russia. A note of urgency was added in 1884 when the Russians occupied the oasis at Merv, halfway between Khiva and the mountainous northern reaches of Afghanistan. The following year the Russians attacked Afghan forces in the border zone at Penjdeh, and Britain and Russia came to the brink of war. Open conflict was averted through diplomacy, but Rawlinson's long-held view that a head-on clash was inevitable seemed to have been vindicated.

But by this time the main focus of attention of the RGS had moved elsewhere. Africa was now the Society's grand obsession, and in the early 1870s all eyes were on David Livingstone during his last travels in the continent that he had done so much to unwrap and decode. In 1876 Leopold II, king of Belgium, invited representatives from the RGS to a conference in Brussels. Its purpose was to consider the scientific exploration and economic development of central Africa. The Society sent Rawlinson and the incumbent President Sir Rutherford Alcock. Neither was an expert on Africa, but both had practical experience of the involvement of the RGS with African exploration.[9]

Congo Officers in Council 1880.
Back row (left to right): Dr
R. Leslie, Mr E. Glave, Lt. J. N.
Hurt, Major Parminter, Captain
J. Grant Elliot, Mr A. B.
Swinburn and Major F. R. Vetch.
Seated in centre (left to right):
Colonel Sir F. De Winton and
Mr H. M. Stanley.

Other British attendees were Sir Bartle Frere, Sir Leopold Heath, Sir Thomas Fowell Buxton, William Mackinnon, Sir Harry Verney and Sir John Kennaway. They were all interested in missionary work and in abolishing the slave trade. Two explorers with recent experience in Africa were also invited: Colonel James Grant and Commander V. L. Cameron. At the conference Alcock presented King Leopold with a map of Africa.

The king, in his address, spoke of the need to eliminate the slave trade from Africa, and to promote its cultural and commercial development. To this end he presented a blueprint for the future of Africa. It was a vision of a kind of benign bureaucracy, to be installed and managed by the European powers. He proposed the establishment of a series of "scientific stations" for the purpose of promoting research and cultural advancement. It was agreed that four such stations should be set up across central Africa, and that they would be administered by an international commission—the International African Association. In each of the European nations committed to the project, there would be national committees charged with raising funds and organizing projects for exploration and development.

After the conference the RGS set up a committee to look into ways of supporting the king's grand design. The Society decided against a formal link, not wishing to ally itself too closely with an organization that looked as if it might be the political tool of a foreign power. Initially, neither the Foreign Office nor the Colonial Office voiced any unease about the Association, but concerns were raised after the Prince of Wales was approached by King Leopold and asked to chair the British National Committee. This raised the possibility that the heir to the throne, along with British delegates to the International Association, might face the indignity of being out-voted on matters of political importance to the state and the crown. The prince declined King Leopold's request, and the RGS set up its own African Exploration Fund in 1877.

The RGS did not entirely avoid controversy over its involvement with King Leopold's plan. In the archives there is a letter, dated July 21, 1877, from Sir Rutherford Alcock to Sir Thomas Biddulph, Queen Victoria's Keeper of the Privy Purse[10], written to allay the Queen's concern "that her relative King Leopold was being slighted by the RGS and her eldest son".[11] Alcock did his best, with much exaggerated deference, to set Her Majesty's mind at rest on that score. At the same time he gently and obsequiously made the case for Britain's political and economic involvement in Africa. "New markets have to be sought if we are to sustain our individual pre-eminence," he said, "and these can only be found in countries still occupied by scarce populations of semi-civilized or quite barbarous races."

Alcock then promoted the RGS's own fund as the best way to keep up with other European nations in the race to reap the benefits of African exploration: "It was from this point of view that I desired to obtain Her Majesty's approval of the action of the Geographical Society, and its Exploration Fund Committee, which is organizing the means whereby England may assume its appropriate place in a movement the sovereigns of Europe no less than the people of each country are now actively promoting. Her Majesty's loyal subjects are naturally anxious that the Queen's name should be associated with whatever work is destined to bring either glory or benefit to the nation. The past history of the fruitful results of African exploration by British geographers in the last quarter of a century, by which the vast lake regions and river systems of the interior have been made known to the world, show such possibilities of development and national wealth in the near future of Africa that all are eager to advance."

There were, in other words, better ways for Britain to achieve the scientific and free-trade components of Leopold's aims. Especially because the king's plans were soon to have tragic consequences. It emerged that in the Belgian-administered territory of Congo, African workers, who were forced to gather natural rubber, were subjected to horrific punishments for failing to meet their quotas. The scandal deeply undermined support for the International Association.

The whole episode affected the Royal Geographical Society too. It now viewed with suspicion any undertaking that smacked too much of politics. The historian R. C. Bridges has written that "the Society consciously shied away from non-scientific pursuits in relation to Africa after a little experience of them in relation to Leopold II's ideas. It was not, like its counterpart in Paris, a centre where those interested in schemes for overseas expansion foregathered to plan their campaigns, and it was even less like the numerous 'commercial geography' societies which in the 1870s and 1880s sprang up in many parts of Europe."[12]

So, although the high officials of the Society might have expressed a view on Anglo-Russian politics or have taken an interest in the partition of Africa, useful geographical science remained its root and its *raison d'être*. This stance reflected the pragmatic, dutiful outlook of many of its Fellows. "The whole society was composed in such a way as to make it a natural forum for the administrators, engineers, surveyors, soldiers and sailors who worked around the world in Britain's interest," wrote Bridges. "It may not be too much to say that the very practical geography which interested them was a 'scientific superstructure' on a commercial middle-class economic base."[13]

THE BUSINESS OF EXPLORATION

This geographical spadework had to be done in the field, and by the middle of the 19th century the RGS was well established as a promoter and supporter of foreign expeditions. Once again, it was Africa that proved the most fertile ground. "In the second half of the century, the Dark Continent was to replace the Antipodes as the premier laboratory of archaic conditions," Stafford has written. "Here, more intensely than anywhere else, the explorer acted out the European longing to be challenged by nature in a wild and exotic setting. In so doing, he simultaneously verified the superiority of European civilisation, opened new frontiers for expansive capitalism, and provided an outlet for emotional impulses stifled by industrialisation and urbanisation."[14]

The Society's support was often straightforwardly financial, and it was not always possible to keep a tight rein on the budget. The explorer Verney Lovett Cameron, in his journey across central Africa between 1873 and 1875, incurred costs

"Stanley's Hot Goal" from the magazine 'Rare Bits', November 15 1890. The cartoon illustrates the intensity of criticism directed at Stanley's methods of exploration and his scientific writings.

STANLEY'S HOT GOAL.

that amounted to £11,000—far more than was agreed. The Treasury was persuaded to donate £3,000 toward Cameron's outgoings after the event. But the Society could at least try to insist on value for money. These instructions, given in a letter of 1860 from the RGS Secretary to Captain J. H. Speke, read like a rather severely worded contract:

"The Royal Geographical Society, having determined to send an expedition to Eastern Africa, hereby appoint you to the command of the same, with Captn Grant as Assistant, who in the event of any accident occurring to yourself, of a nature to deprive the expedition of your services, is empowered to succeed you.

"The chief object of this expedition is to determine the locality whence the head waters of the White Nile take their rise. For this purpose, you are to travel without delay to the southern limit of Lake Nyanza, and to continue your exploration northwards. It is also hoped that you may find it practicable to make a short exploration of the northern limits, and the water drainage of the Karagwah Mountains, in case an affluent of the Nile should take its rise from them.

"You are to determine the northern limits of the Nyanza and to ascertain whether or not its waters have any communication with the White Nile. You are also as far as may be possible, without serious delay and without compromising the safety of the Expedition, to examine the physical features of the whole contour of this remarkable lake. That is to say, to determine the number and positions of its chief tributaries and its outlet, the depth and elevation of its waters and the axial direction and dips of the adjacent mountain chains. Finally, you are to endeavour to reach Gondokoro on the White Nile, reputed to be in Lat. 4° 52' N."[15]

The document goes on to give Speke leave to return by whatever route is deemed appropriate. It also invites him to gather information on physical features, tribes and the commercial opportunities of the region, and gives instructions on drawing and accounting for the money granted by the RGS. Strict advice is given about the prior rights of the RGS over information gained from the expedition. Speke and Grant travelled more than 4,000 miles (6,400 km) in Africa. On their way back, perhaps mindful of their rigid contractual obligations, they cabled ahead to London that "the Nile is settled".

It was not in fact settled at all. Speke was claiming that Lake Victoria was the source, but he was only hazarding a guess. Lake Albert, 150 miles (240 km) to the northwest, was just as likely a candidate, as many people pointed out. Speke continued to argue his case. In 1864 he agreed to take part in a debate on the subject of the source of the Nile in the presence of David Livingstone. But the day before—in an accident that has never been satisfactorily explained—John Speke shot himself dead. Thirteen years later it transpired that he had been right all along: Lake Victoria was indeed the source of the Nile.

For all the changes wrought from within and without, the Royal Geographical Society retained the conservative character of a gentlemen's club throughout its first decades. Women were not admitted to the Society, and there was no acknowledgment of the role that Africans played in the "discovery" of their own lands.

That supercilious view of the business of exploration began to change in the 1870s. After the death of Livingstone, for example, the Society did its best to acknowledge the feat of the two Africans—James Chuma and Abdullah Susi—who carried the explorer's body to the coast and accompanied it back to England. And in 1875 a few forward-thinking souls made the first, failed attempt to raise the issue of the admission of women as Fellows. In 1892 the President formally proposed to the Council that women be eligible for election to Fellowship. But this process fell foul of a number of dissenting male Fellows, and the proposal was lost. It was not until 1913, well into the wider struggle for female suffrage, that women geographers and explorers were finally given equal rights within the Society's walls.[16]

The contribution of black Africans to exploration was somehow invisible in the 19th century, although the great British triumphs—the deeds of Africanists such as Speke, Grant, Burton, Livingstone, Cameron and Stanley—would have been impossible without the help of indigenous peoples. They travelled just as far as their European employers, and endured all

A caricature of Sir Henry Creswicke Rawlinson K.C.B by Sir Leslie Ward (otherwise known as 'Spy') from the 12th July 1873 edition of Vanity Fair. The picture was originally titled "Statesmen, No. 147–Our Eastern Policy."

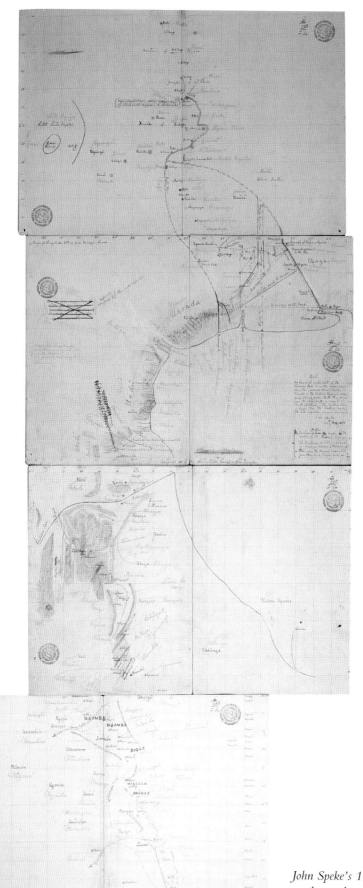

A photograph of John Hanning Speke (1827–1864) taken in 1859.

John Speke's 1864 map of the northwest shores of Victoria Nyanza, the source of the Nile and the Ripon Falls.

"Moobarik Bombay"
who has accompanied Cap.ⁿ Speke during 2 Expeditions in Central Africa.

J. A. Grant's stereo prints of "Moobarik Bombay" from 1860. Born around 1820 and enslaved as a child, Bombay was taken to India, then returned to Africa in the service of the Sultan of Zanzibar. He later served the Burton and Speke expedition in 1859, and Speke's expedition in 1860, in which he acted as interpreter and negotiator. He travelled with Stanley in his search for Livingstone, and accompanied V. L. Cameron on his trans-African journey. In 1876 he was given a pension by the RGS. He died in October 1885.

Below: White Rhinoceros and African Rhinocerous by John Speke in 1862.

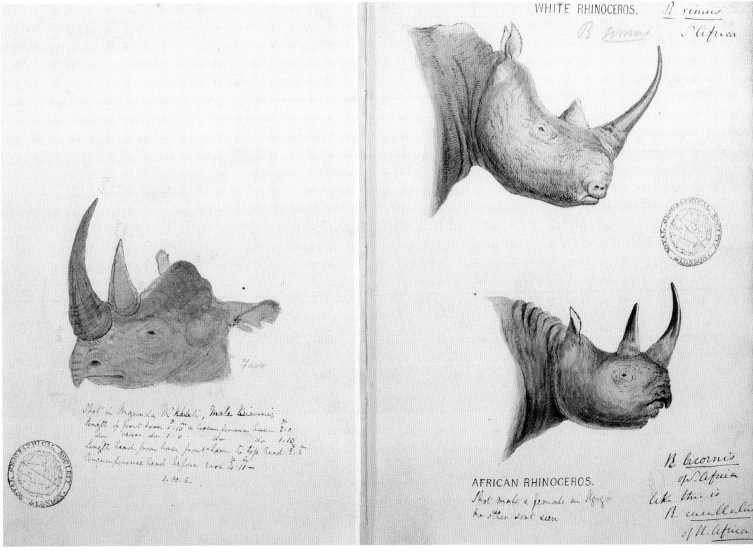

the same hardships. It has been suggested that 350 or more porters were required for large expeditions in East Africa, where tsetse flies and malarial mosquitos made the use of pack animals impossible. Local men carried everything that the expedition required: arms, scientific and camping equipment, food and gifts.[17]

The term "porter" does not do justice to their work. Their contributions included essential useful insider knowledge of the local territory; some worked as translators from Swahili and other African languages; they also performed a vital function as negotiators with local chieftains. Speke, for example, had little knowledge of the languages spoken in the areas where he travelled—on his expedition of 1860–63 he left much of the discussion with tribal chiefs to his headmen, two Africans named Bombay and Baraka.[18]

FROM FIELDWORK TO PAPERWORK

All the mass of information and knowledge gathered on expeditions would be funnelled back to the RGS, and ultimately presented to the Society and the world in the form of publications. The written output of the RGS included its periodical book publications, the records of its meetings and public debates, the vast archives of minutes of meetings, committee notes, correspondence, and—particularly revealing—the personal journals of explorers and Society officials.

The Society also published a journal, the first two volumes of which appeared in 1832. From 1855 to 1978 accounts of meetings and other affairs were made known through the Society's *Proceedings*. Both these publications were deemed by some to be rather dry. The Honorary Secretary of the RGS, Clements Markham, dissatisfied with the RGS's existing publications, privately launched a new monthly journal—at first entitled *Ocean Highways: the Geographical Record* and then renamed *The Geographical Magazine*, whose copyright was purchased by the RGS in 1878. In 1879 a redesigned *Proceedings* was launched—now cumbersomely entitled *Proceedings of the Royal Geographical Society and Monthly Record of Geography*. It continued until 1892, when it was replaced by *The Geographical Journal*, which is published to the present day.

From 1898 onward, a *Year-Book* and *Record* of the RGS was published. Markham, in his preface to the first edition, hoped that the information provided "will lead to more frequent visits to their rooms, and to a largely increased use of the geographical treasures they contain,"—an aim remarkably similar to that of the "Unlocking the Archives" project.

David Livingstone's coffin in the Map Room of the Royal Geographical Society's headquarters at 1 Savile Row, London, before being taken to Westminster Abbey.

The RGS also produced special publications, the most important of which was its *Hints to Travellers*. This 31-page work was first printed in 1854 as part of the journal, and was concerned with the use of instruments for field observation. It was later reissued as a separate volume, and over the next 90 years was revised and reprinted time and again. An eighth edition, now in two volumes, was produced in 1901. The 10th edition comprised 788 pages and the 11th, reprinted at the end of the Second World War, was an immense 890 pages long: more of an encyclopedia than a book of hints. Volume One, with 448 pages, has detailed information on surveying, field astronomy instruments and mapping, and Volume Two, with 472 pages, has instructions for the setting-up of camps for scientific observation, and first-aid practices for the treatment of various types of injury and disease. Both books contain commercial advertisements.

At the end of the 19th century the RGS was as interested in maps as it was in words. Much time and effort was devoted to acquiring material from government agencies such as the War Office and the Colonial Office—some of it highly sensitive—and drawing maps based on it. These maps were used to illustrate papers published in the various organs of the RGS and as visual aids in evening talks. Field surveys by explorers were also worked up into usable maps. In the early days these maps were produced by outside companies, but by the last decade of the century the Society was employing its own cartographers. These in-house map-makers continued to produce maps for publication into the 1970s.

Despite the vast amount of activity undertaken by the RGS, geography was still not seen as an important field of study in schools and universities. Campaigning for proper geographical education at all levels—up to and including the civil service and the armed forces—became an important part of the RGS's function. In 1884 the Society appointed John Keltie to conduct a special enquiry into geographical education. He went to France and Germany to see how the subject was taught there, and found that Britain was woefully inadequate by comparison. He advised the RGS to make every attempt to improve geographical education through advocacy, modest funding, prizes and exhibitions of geographical "apparatus".[19]

In 1885, the year Keltie delivered his verdict, the geographer E. G. Ravenstein gave a lecture to the Society. In it he said: "I am quite willing to admit that the hours spent upon geographical instruction might be employed to better purpose if our aim be merely to crowd the memory with barren names of places, and to impact a knowledge of their positions by means of a map. The Council of the Royal Geographical Society maintains, however, that the teaching of geography possesses a high educational value, quite apart from its more directly practical bearings, and I hope to show that in the hands of competent teachers it may become a most efficient instrument for training the intellectual powers."[20]

The RGS lobbied universities, urging them to introduce geography into their teaching. A hint of the Society's frustration is to be found in an 1886 letter written by its President, Lord Aberdare, to the Vice-Chancellor at Oxford. "The Council of the Royal Geographical Society have on two previous occasions addressed memorials to your Predecessors, urging the claims of Geography to further recognition in the universities," wrote Aberdare. "So much of human knowledge and human interests is bound up with the relations and interaction of the physical conditions of the earth, the study of which is practically embraced in Geography, that there are few branches of Education which do not present a geographical aspect, and which do not therefore offer a field for instruction in Geography in combination with some other subject."[21]

The letter goes on to point out that geography already held a "statutable place" at Oxford. A paper in Historical Geography was offered in the Final Honour School of Modern History. Aberdare says that the appointment of a reader or professor would be the next logical step, and states that the RGS would be prepared to help finance such a post. This approach was successful, and in 1887 Oxford created a Readership in Geography. Cambridge followed suit in 1888.

By the end of the 19th century the RGS was established as a leading scientific society. Its contribution to science was widely recognized, and its meetings were well supported. The 1898 *Year Book* gives a flavour of the Society's business and character on the eve of a new age. In that year there were 3,929 Fellows, the highest total since its foundation. The listed interests of the Fellows were widely spread. Those of Halford Mackinder, the first Reader of Geography at Oxford, are given as educational geography and historical geography. Sir Clements Markham's are "Arctic, Peru, Abyssinia, India, Pacific, and comparative geography". In the lists of "referees arranged according to subjects", the dominant areas are the Arctic, Asia and Africa, with fewer names attached to Europe, North and South America, Australasia and the Pacific. Thematic subjects include astronomical geography, cartography, physical geography (including geology), historical and critical geography, education, orthography, bibliography and general geography.

These lists add up to a vast field of expertise and scholarship. In 70 years, the Royal Geographical Society had come a long way from those dining clubs in Pall Mall and St. James's. But a long century of change and upheaval still lay ahead.

Diagram of a sextant and instructions on how to use it from the first volume of Hints to Travellers (eighth edition), 'Surveying and Practical Astronomy', from 1901.

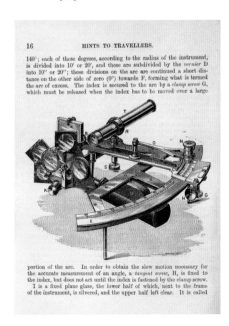

NEW HORIZONS: THE RGS AND THE IBG IN THE 20TH CENTURY

Robin Butlin

At the dawn of the 20th century, an English person did not need to be an explorer in order to see strange new sights. The world was changing rapidly, and no place on earth was more mutable and exotic than London, the "mighty heart" of the British Empire. In this city, and elsewhere around the globe, a technological revolution was under way, and the appearance of new modes of transport was its most obvious manifestation. The petrol engine looked set to transform short daily journeys across town, and the first aircraft were soon to make it possible to travel swiftly—if not entirely safely—across seas and national frontiers.

H. R. Mill, writing in 1930 about the history of the RGS, described the cityscape in which the Society was physically located on the eve of these developments. The long urban dominance of the horse-drawn cab was coming to an end: "The general use of solid rubber tyres had at last brought smooth perfection to the hansom cab, that ubiquitous gondola of London, which was gliding all unsuspected straight to its long home in a museum. Pneumatic tyres and the chain-geared safety bicycle wrought a revolution in those years which set everyone on wheels, and for a time the pedal cycle was the fastest machine on the road, passing all else and passed by none."[1]

The winds of change were blowing through London, and gusting down Savile Row too. Mill has this to say about the new mores within the Society: "The formality of dress manners … drew to its close. [In the nineteenth century] few gentlemen ventured to appear at any afternoon function save in a frock-coat and silk hat; but at the dawn of the twentieth century an under-current of rebellion began to set against the tide of convention, and the sudden currency of the adjective *fin-de-siècle* betokened an awakening to the imminence of changes in mental attitude as well as in external conditions."[2]

Previous page: members of the Peru-Bolivia Boundary Commission (1911-13) walk through the lowlands of Peru during their research.

George Henry's portrait of Sir Clements Markham, RGS Honorable Secretary 1863–88 and President 1893–1905.

SIR CLEMENTS MARKHAM: FATHER OF ANTARCTIC RESEARCH

At the RGS, the years spanning the turn of the century were presided over by Sir Clements Markham (1830-1916). He was a remarkable administrator and reformer who served as honorary secretary of the Society for 25 years, between 1863 and 1888, before becoming President in 1893 at the age of 63.

But Markham was no desk-bound bureaucrat: Foreign adventure had been part of his life from a young age. He joined the navy at the age of 14, and while still in his teens he took part in one of the 40 expeditions that sought the explorer John Franklin and his crew. They had mysteriously gone missing while in search of the so-called "Northwest Passage" from the Atlantic to the Pacific via the icy archipelago of Upper Canada. Franklin and all his men were dead long before anyone reached them—but it was the expedition on *HMS Assistance*, in which Markham took part, that found the records of the voyage. Franklin's men had buried them inside a cairn before they died of scurvy.

After leaving the navy at the age of 22, Markham went to Peru, where he spent a year examining Inca sites and other ancient settlements. In 1858 he joined the Revenue Department of the India Office. This newly created ministry was a kind of Foreign Office dedicated to the sub-continent. It had been set up in the wake of the Indian Mutiny (Great

Map, above, of the Arctic
exploration that provided
the first information about Sir John
Franklin's missing party. It was
published accompanying an article
by Dr. John Rae entitled 'Arctic
Exploration, with Information
respecting Sir John Franklin's
missing Party' in the Journal
of the Royal Geographical
Society, *Vol. 25, 1855. The
sketch of Tennyson's Monument,
left, in Greenland is by Dr. Elisha
Kent Kane. Kane named the rock
formation after the English poet.*

Map of the
ARCTIC EXPLORATION.
from which resulted the first information of
Sir John Franklin's missing Party;
by
Dr John Rae.
1854.

Rebellion) of 1857, in which indigenous soldiers had sparked a widespread uprising against British rule. The revolt was suppressed, and the East India Company, which effectively ruled India, was abolished. The India Office, which answered directly to the minister in London, was installed in its place. It was in this politically sensitive organ of state that Markham's administrative skills were first put to the test. He brought all his energy to bear on the job, and pointed out the deplorable state of the new department's records and maps.

In 1859 the India Office sent the 29-year-old Markham back to Peru to collect various species of the cinchona tree, the bark of which contains quinine and so protects against malaria. The plan was to propagate these so-called "fever-bark trees" in India. It was a dangerous expedition, but Markham and others succeeded in gathering seeds and getting them out of the country. However, most of the specimens collected by Markham did not survive the voyage to England, and the rest were dead before they reached India. Later specimens collected by other British plant-hunters were brought safely to the sub-continent, and the next challenge was to grow the cinchona trees successfully. So, in 1860 Markham returned to India to supervise the planting. It took some experimentation, but the Peruvian fever-bark trees were eventually persuaded to grow on Indian soil. In 1867, seven years after Markham's Peruvian expedition, Indian cinchona plantations covered 1200 acres.[3]

By that time Markham was on his travels again. The India Office appointed him geographer to a military foray into the kingdom of Abyssinia. This mission, led by Lord Napier, was charged with forcing King Theodore III to release English representatives he had taken hostage. Markham was with British troops when they joined battle with the Abyssinian army at Magdala. The Abyssinians were defeated, the king shot himself, and the hostages were freed.

A flag for the RGS designed by Sir Clements Markham and flown from the roof at Savile Row in 1895. Markham later recalled in his diary (1902–06) that "I should have preferred a correct swallow tailed standard … but people would not have understood it."

Markham returned to the India Office where, in recognition of his achievements as a traveller and an administrator, he was made head of the Geographical Department. He left government service in the 1870s and devoted himself to writing. He produced works on the history of exploration, studies of Peru and its people, a book entitled *Peruvian Bark* about the life-saving cinchona, and various books on his own family history. In 1875 he joined his brother, Commander Albert Markham, on a voyage to the Arctic areas of Greenland. After years of work in the sweltering climes of India and South America, he found himself once again on the icy topknot of the world. The trip seems to have rekindled his interest in the colder parts of the world—as President of the RGS he became "the father of modern Antarctic research" and the driving force behind the British exploration of this little-known continent.

Markham took up the presidency of the RGS in 1893, and kept a journal all the time he was in the post. This journal is a record of his own life and that of the Society at a critical time. It highlights issues that engaged the President and other officers and Fellows of the RGS, and gives an idea of the kind of reforms Markham was considering. One of his concerns, for example, was to make sure that the expertise of the members of the council covered all regions of the globe.

Markham's journal also provides an insight into his management style, which seems to owe something to his time in the Royal Navy. "In July 1895 I caused a flag staff to be set up on the roof [of 1 Savile Row], with a flag, to be hoisted on days of Council Meetings, and official occasions. It is the Union Jack with the Society's badge in the centre."[4]

Paintings of polar exploration: a canoe (left) broaching to in a gale at sunrise from the book Narrative of a journey to the shores of the Polar Sea, in 1819–22 *by Sir John Franklin. Below: the British Arctic Expedition, led by Sir George Strong Nares, was an attempt to reach the North Pole via Smith Sound. Although the men did not reach the Pole, they did explore the coasts of Greenland and adjacent lands in their ships,* HMS Alert *and* HMS Discovery *and returned with vast amounts of geographical and scientific data.*

At the turn of the 20th century the opportunities for exploration were decreasing. So the biggest question facing the Society during Markham's presidency was: where to go next? Now that the blanks on the map of Africa were rapidly being filled, which parts of the world remained to be explored? To Markham the answer was clear—in fact it had been in his mind for some time. He directed the gaze of the RGS south, toward the vast, inimical, and apparently featureless massif of Antarctica.

The Antarctic was not an entirely unknown quantity. In the 18th and early-19th centuries seal-hunters had gained a knowledge of its cold periphery, and the hunters were soon followed by formal scientific expeditions from Britain and France. From 1839 to 1843 a British team under Sir James Clark Ross extended the knowledge and mapping of Antarctica. Ross's expedition cut through the pack ice in two specially strengthened ships, the *Erebus* and the *Terror*. They reached a point 78° 10' south, deep inside the huge continental bay that is now called the Ross Sea. This was as far south as anyone had ever been, and is about as close as one can get to the South Pole without disembarking and continuing overland.

Sixty years on, Markham decided that the time was now right for a new investigation of the Antarctic. Together with John Murray, a leading academic authority on the poles, he sought to persuade other scientific societies to back an Antarctic expedition. In 1895, the Sixth International Geographical Congress, held on Markham's home territory in London, passed a resolution stating that "the exploration of the Antarctic regions is the greatest piece of geographical exploration still to be undertaken."

Now it remained only to raise the money to recruit and equip an expedition. Markham lobbied for cash as hard as he could, but got nowhere. It looked like the honour of opening up Antarctica would fall to other nations until an unexpected breakthrough came from within the Society. In 1899 Llewellyn Longstaff, a Fellow of the RGS and a successful businessman, donated £25,000 to start the Antarctic project. This was enough to begin construction of a purpose-built ship, which was named the *Discovery*. Markham also now picked the man he wanted to lead the expedition: a naval lieutenant by the name of Robert Falcon Scott.

The project came to fruition in 1901. Scott and his team spent two long winters in the Antarctic, and amassed a huge amount of information and experience. They also penetrated further south than Ross, setting a new record. But *Discovery*, meanwhile, became frozen at anchor, deep inside the ice shelf. When it was time to head for home Scott's men had to laboriously dynamite a channel through the ice so that the ship could reach the open sea. It was a tough end to a hard expedition, but it was also a fine success. Scott arrived home in 1904.

Three years later one of Scott's officers, Ernest Shackleton, led another expedition to Antarctica. In the course of a nightmarish expedition Shackleton marched to a point 88° 23' south—within 100 miles (160 km) of the magnetic South Pole. His party then made a desperate dash back to the north. Shackleton had set a date when the ship's party were to

The sorrow and the beauty:
Scott's party, below, look
despondent as they stand by the
tent of Roald Amundsen at the
South Pole (the Norwegian team
had reached the Pole days earlier).
From left to right Titus Oates,

Robert Falcon Scott, E. A. Wilson
and E. R. Evans. None of them
returned from the 800-mile
journey. Right, Herbert Ponting's
image, of a tear-shaped grotto in
an iceberg during the Terra Nova
Expedition 1910–13.

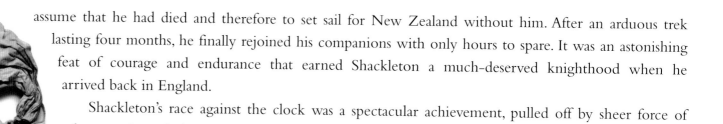

Bag of provisions found at Captain Scott's last camp on the British Antarctic Expedition 1910–13, and now kept in the RGS archive. The bags contain tea, curry and salt, and are sealed with wax.

assume that he had died and therefore to set sail for New Zealand without him. After an arduous trek lasting four months, he finally rejoined his companions with only hours to spare. It was an astonishing feat of courage and endurance that earned Shackleton a much-deserved knighthood when he arrived back in England.

Shackleton's race against the clock was a spectacular achievement, pulled off by sheer force of character. It made him a national hero. But Markham did not like the man at all, and he was glad to see his old protégé Robert Scott appointed to lead the third Antarctic expedition. This journey has entered the rich mythology of British history. Scott reached the South Pole, but found when he got there that he had been beaten to it by the Norwegian explorer Roald Amundsen. Scott and his party died on the way back. This tale of a heroic failure was romanticized in subsequent re-telling until it became a kind of parable of British fortitude. But the rosy legend came later. At the time of his death, there was only sadness and grief. Markham made this rather bitter entry in his journal when he heard of it: "The appalling news came that Scott had reached the South Pole on January 8th 1912, but that he and all his party had perished in a furious gale on their return journey ... Even now I can hardly believe it. There has passed away, if it is really true, a very exceptionally noble Englishman. What struck me most was his chivalrous generosity in dealing with contemptible self seekers such as Shackleton and Amundsen. Very rarely have so many qualities been combined in one man."[5]

Even after the Antarctic expeditions there was still anxiety about the dearth of areas available for European exploration and settlement. This was a common theme of lectures and maps published in *The Geographical Journal*. D. G. Hogarth, in a 1908 paper on western Asia, identified three areas, mainly in the Arabian peninsula, that were still unknown to Europeans. Another paper in *The Geographical Journal* in 1911 by F . R. Cana, an expert on Africa, described the few zones of that continent, apart from the Sahara, that were as yet unmapped in one way or another. These included areas in the Congo Basin, Kenya and Ethiopia.[6]

CHANGES OF PLACE AND BOUNDARIES

By now Markham had passed on the presidency of the Society. His successors continued to make changes—of which the most visible was the relocation of the Society to a new building. In 1912 Lord Curzon (President of the RGS from 1911 to 1914) learned that Lowther Lodge, on Kensington Gore opposite Hyde Park, was for sale. The house had been designed and built between 1872 and 1875 in the Queen Anne style by Richard Norman Shaw. He was the architect of many London landmarks, including the Piccadilly Hotel, the Gaiety Theatre and New Scotland Yard. Curzon moved energetically to purchase the building for the RGS. The Society paid £100,000 to acquire it, and spent a further £6,000 on refurbishment (1 Savile Row was sold for £38,000). The Society's new home was opened for use on 14 April 1913.

The new site was significant in other ways too. L. Walker, a historian of the Society's buildings, has drawn attention to the fact that Lowther Lodge is "in the midst of Kensington, surrounded by the highest concentration of significant cultural symbols of Victorian England, the Albert Hall, the Albert Memorial, and the museums and colleges of South Kensington."[7] This part of the city was, and remains, a kind of university campus, where ideas and knowledge are the common currency.

But there was also a symbolism in leaving behind the gentlemen's club on Savile Row. H. R. Mill, in his work celebrating the centenary of the Society, wrote that: "The introduction of tube railways and the universal use of motor buses and taxicabs had banished from Kensington Gore the bogey of inaccessibility, and the advance of public opinion had also removed the prejudice against the admission of women as Fellows."[8] In other words, it is no coincidence that the ban of women was finally lifted in the same year that the Society made its home in a new building in a new part of London.

Views of Lowther Lodge, clockwise from top left. The wall and the original wooden gates of the lodge in 1882; the Museum Room in 1920; the main hall of the Royal Geographical Society (with IBG) as it is today; the Society's Library in 1930.

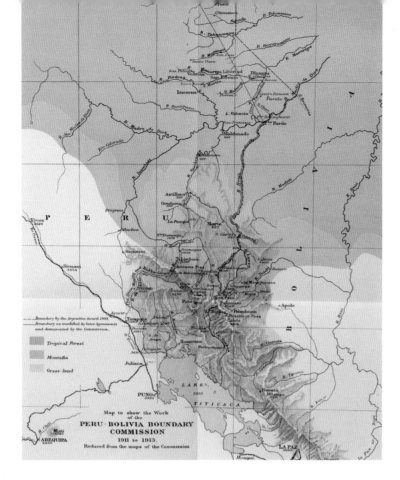

Map, right, showing the work of the Peru-Bolivia Boundary Commission (1911–13) for which the RGS nominated the survey officers and published the resulting maps and report. Far right, members of the commission build a wooden trigonometrical station.

Opposite: A member of the Peru-Bolivia Boundary Commission takes readings from the mountainside near Lake Trapiche, Peru.

Not that everyone approved. Markham, in the journal that he still kept, wrote in high dudgeon of the "ruin of the Royal Geographical Society", saying that "at Lowther Lodge there is a smoking room, writing room, tearoom for ladies—a sort of suburban club. They are filling the Society with women. The finances are in confusion, all our investments spent and £20,000 borrowed. Nothing for geography. Their hope is to make it up, by selling part of the gardens at Lowther Lodge … I look upon the Society as ruined: turned into a suburban smoking club for suffragettes."[9]

These profound changes occurred at a time when the world at large was in a state of flux. When war broke out in 1914, the geographical expertise of the RGS became a valuable asset. Although the Society was less directly bound up with the war effort than, say, the Société de Géographie de Paris, nonetheless, as M. Heffernan has shown, some 50 handbooks and reports were drawn up using the map libraries and other holdings of the RGS and the Admiralty. Maps of Asia and Europe were prepared at a scale of 1:1 million by staff at the RGS, and were used as the basis for territorial boundary determinations at the Paris Peace Conference at Versailles.[10]

The resources of the RGS were also made available to government departments during the First World War. An index of GSGS (Geographical Section of the General Staff) maps of Belgium and France was compiled, as was a map of Britain in four sheets at a scale of 1:500,000. The work was done by women volunteers from Cheltenham Ladies' College and London University, under the supervision of the RGS's in-house cartographer. D. G. Hogarth[11], the council member who had identified Arabia as a future focus of European exploration, contributed to the production of detailed maps of Turkey and the Middle East. Along with his protégé T. E. Lawrence, he is thought to have been part of a British intelligence group gathering information on German activity in the Middle East.

During the Second World War, the links between geography and warfare continued. Geographers were involved, as Hugh Clout and Cyril Gosme have shown, in the production in Oxford and Cambridge of the many volumes of the Naval Intelligence Division's *Geographical Handbook* series.[12] These provided geographical knowledge of theatres of war and adjacent regions, and provided a basis for strategic planning. The wider role of geographers in the Second World War was the object of a project organized on behalf of the RGS by W. G. V. Balchin, the summary findings of which were reported in *The Geographical Journal* in 1987.[13]

The flurry of map-making activity after the First World War drew on the Society's long experience of boundary surveys. Much important fieldwork was done in Africa at the end of the "scramble" when the British, French, Belgians, Germans, and Portuguese were marking out their separate territories. In her book *The Africa House,* the writer Christina Lamb wryly describes the frustrating experiences of one British officer working with the Anglo-Belgian Boundary Commission as it endeavoured to define the border between Northern Rhodesia and the Congo in the years just before the outbreak of the Great War.

Lamb wrote: "The Anglo-Belgian Boundary Commission … was just all far too bureaucratic and tied up with the petty egos of other officers. Within three months Captain Everett, the second-in-command, was eaten by a lion, a most ill-omened start. Major Gillam, who headed the Commission, spent most of his time in a haze of whisky and kept issuing and rescinding orders, the loneliness of the African bush finally driving him to a complete breakdown. At the end, his senior officer Major Steel had pocketed the finishing bonus for the natives."[14]

The Society's reputation was such that it was sometimes asked by foreign governments to help with the survey, mapping, and arbitration of their international boundaries. In 1911, for example, the Society received a request from the Republic of Peru, Markham's old haunt, to carry out the demarcation of the boundary between Peru and Bolivia. The introduction to the resulting report is by Sir Thomas Holdich, President of the RGS from 1917 to 1919 and a major authority on boundary arbitration. He had been a survey officer on India's Northwest Frontier in his youth, and served on the Pamir Boundary Commission from 1884 to 1886. During the First World War, when European borders were constantly shifting and crumbling under the weight of the world's armies, he published a timely book entitled *Political Frontiers and Boundary Making.*[15]

A different kind of cartographical service was provided by the draughtsmen in the Society's map-drawing room. They performed the invaluable function of creating accurate maps from the sketches and mass of readings and measurements brought back by explorers from far-off places. This was a kind of geographical code-breaking: turning roughly scribbled figures and numbers into something more visually comprehensible.

The draughtsmen's duties included producing maps for meetings and for publication in the *Journal* and *Proceedings*, proof-reading, and assisting with pointing out features on maps used at lectures. This work was directed by a series of interesting and able cartographers. The look of the maps naturally changed over time, but some very distinctive house styles evolved. These included the use of quill-pen lettering and strong framing of map borders, which was introduced by RGS secretary A. R. Hinks. This style met with some criticism, and gave way after the Second World War to modern printed and transferred lettering styles, but while it lasted it lent an aesthetic quality to the Society's maps.[16]

Above, a 1906 photograph of Captain Thomas Holdich (later President of the RGS, 1917–19) and Captain McSweeney in Afghanistan. The image is taken from the report of the Pamir Boundary Commission of 1897.

Among the explorers who provided raw data to the Society's cartographers were the Arabists Gertrude Bell and William Shakespear. Their dog-eared and sand-blasted notebooks are in the archive. At the time that they were roaming the desert, during and after the First World War, there was a subtle shift in notions of exploration, and a questioning of its aims. The nature of the papers published in *The Geographical Journal* at this time suggest that expeditions were increasingly linked to narrow objectives: politics was one; others included such scientific disciplines as ornithology. There was also a growing interest in the study of anthropology. Major anthropological expeditions, modelled on the journeys of A. C. Haddon in the Torres Strait from 1898–1899, were undertaken by Cooke Daniell, C. G. Seligman, and W. M. Strong around the Gulf of Papua in New Guinea in 1904.[17]

"THE MOST VIGOROUS GEOGRAPHICAL SOCIETY IN EUROPE"

New subject areas and new approaches in both human and physical geography were being promoted in British universities in the 1920s and 1930s. These new areas were, naturally enough, mostly the preserve of younger geographers, many of whom were Fellows of the RGS. This difference in outlook was one factor that led to internal stresses within the RGS. A generation gap was about to make itself felt.

At the end of the 1920s there was gathering discontent among younger academic Fellows of the RGS, who were finding it hard to get their papers presented to the RGS or published. They tried to convince the Research Committee of the need for more publication in the fields of human and regional geography, which were among the leading topics in academic geography. But the response of the RGS was unsatisfactory, and consequently a group of members resolved to break away and form their own association. A committee of academic geographers met in York in September 1932, and produced a statement of its aims: "In the matter of publication, investigations at an earlier stage showed that a considerable body of unpublished work exists and the need for finding some outlet for this may fairly be deemed urgent. The Committee wishes it to be made clear that the proposed activities of the Institute, both in the matter of meetings and publication, are not in any sense to be regarded as competing with those of other geographical bodies and journals, but rather as supplementary."[18]

The Royal Geographical Society Map Room at Lowther Lodge during the 1920s.

The Institute of British Geographers was founded in 1933, with an initial membership of 39 people. It began publishing monographs almost straight away. A few titles give an idea of the new fields of geographical research—particularly ecology and human geography—in which the IBG was interested: *The Pastoral Industries of New Zealand* by R. Ogilvie Buchanan (1935); *The Changing Sea-Level* by Henri Baulig (1935); *Land Classification in Dorset* by L. Ellis Tavener (1937); *The Human Geography of Swaziland* by Dorothy M. Doveton (1937); *Some Problems of Society and Environment* by H. J. Fleure (1947); and, somewhat later, *The Human Geography of Southern Chile* by G. J. Butland (1957). *The Transactions of the Institute of British Geographers* was its main journal publication, joined later by *Area*, both of which enjoy outstanding scholarly and scientific reputations. The IBG's activities included lively annual conferences, field excursions, international seminars, and the formation of specialist research groups.

Within a decade or two of its foundation the IBG became an active and energetic learned society, which contributed enormously to the advancement of geography.[19] The Institute was very well served by its many distinguished honorary officers—presidents, secretaries, editors and Council members. But it was not, at least in structure, fully representative of the whole of the geographical community.[20] C. W. J. Withers has noted that, like the RGS, it had few women as officers, that there was a membership bias toward London, and that in its early days there was a preference for conferences within a London-Oxford-Cambridge triangle.[21]

The RGS and the IBG co-existed happily for nearly 60 years. But by the early 1990s there was a feeling in the two institutions (many geographers were members of both) that their strengths might profitably be re-combined into a single learned society. The RGS, as the older organization, had experience of effective links with government departments and international agencies, a sound publications record, and close association with the promotion and logistics of overseas expeditions. It also had, in its staff and archive, a long institutional memory and a unique collection of data.

The IBG, for its part, was more or less homeless. For most of its existence it had a peripatetic administrative base and no permanent headquarters. But it had been profoundly influential in the consolidation and development of geography in institutions of higher education, and had done much to promote original research in all aspects of the discipline. The two organizations shared a sense of alarm about the perceived failure of government to support the teaching of geography in schools, and a separate global concern about the dangers of environmental change and degradation—a process which geographical science had noted and was continuing to document.

Discussions about a merger of the RGS and the IBG began in 1992. There was, at first, apprehension about the loss of identity by the two learned societies, and about possibilities of diminution of traditional strengths. But in the end the question of whether to merge or not came down to a democratic vote. In 1994 a ballot was held on the proposal for a formal agreement to combine the two societies. Seventy per cent of those voting agreed that the merger should take place, and after the necessary constitutional changes were agreed, the new Society came into being in January 1995. Its new official name was The Royal Geographical Society (with the Institute of British Geographers). Notwithstanding the slightly awkward parenthetical structure of this title, the Society seems to have benefited from the transfusion of new blood.

In his presidential address in 1995, Lord Jellicoe said: "This merger is one of the most important steps forward in the long history of our Society. Our Society, indeed, constitutes by far the largest and most vigorous geographical society in Europe, and it is our responsibility to realize its full potential."[22]

The RGS-IBG retained its commitment to the promotion of geography in universities, colleges, schools and among the broader public. The promotion of geographical education was, in any case, a long-standing tradition by now. Geography has grown immensely as a degree subject since the Society first lobbied for a readership at Oxford. The grants that it gave to Oxford and Cambridge to establish the subject there were later extended to three other universities: Manchester, Aberystwyth and Edinburgh. By 1924, the RGS had donated a total of £20,000 to universities, a sum described by Mill as "substantial when viewed from the standpoint of the Society's resources and the large claims upon them, but ludicrously small to have achieved so much".

Mill goes on to say, with full justification, that the Society "worked long and hard to secure the full recognition of the dignity and value of geography as a branch of university education, and its reward has been considerable". Most universities had a geography department, albeit a small one, before the Second World War. And at the end of the 20th century there were 1,600 geographers in university departments teaching about 7,000 honours degree undergraduates.[23]

Some of the Society's present-day educational work is done in collaboration with other geographical societies such as the Geographical Association. The RGS-IBG has been active in campaigning for an increase in the number of geography

Snow shoes (below) belonging to H. W. Tilman used in 1945 in Val di Gare, south of Mount Marmolada. Right, Tilman pictured against the pinnacles of the East Rongbuk Glacier during the Mount Everest Expedition of 1935.

teachers, in producing benchmark statements for geography in higher education, in creating greater access to its archive resources, in initiating many dialogues on environmental change, and in promoting a series of journals and special publications. These include the *Geographical Journal*, *Area*, *Transactions*, *The Geographical Magazine*, *Special Publications*, *Studies in Geography* and the RGS-IBG Book Series.

The Society continues to award medals and prizes for outstanding work in the subject. It has recently instituted the professional qualification of Chartered Geographer. It gives lectures and conducts fieldwork throughout the United Kingdom by means of its regional committees, theatre initiatives and new technological links. It has close links with Research Councils, and retains its long-held position as an international promoter of geography. Its research groups provide active leadership in research, the dissemination of new knowledge and the continuous revelation of new facets of many places and issues around the globe.

It is interesting to take the list of topics covered by the research groups of the RGS-IBG, and compare it with the 1898 inventory of members' interests, quoted at the end of the previous chapter. Among the contemporary subject areas which might have appeared surprising or baffling to a man such as Sir Clements Markham are: biogeography, geography of leisure and tourism, geography of health, post-socialist geographies, women and geography, and planning and environment.

While all this proselytizing of geography and scholarly work has been going on, the RGS has continued to send people out to difficult places so that they can gather new knowledge. Among the outstanding 20th-century journeys in which the RGS played a part were John Rymill's Antarctic expedition of 1934–37; H. W. Tilman's expedition to Everest in 1938; the successful ascent of Everest in 1953; expeditions to British North Greenland in 1952–54; the Commonwealth Trans-Antarctic Expedition in 1957, in which Vivian Fuchs and Edmund Hillary made the first coast-to-coast crossing of the Antarctic; the Royal Society/RGS Matto Grosso Expedition of 1968–69; and the RGS Sarawak Expedition of 1978–79. To these can be added the Wahiba Sands project in Oman (1985–87), the Shoals of Capricorn project in the Indian Ocean off the coast of the Seychelles and Mauritius (1998–2001) and many others. All these expeditions have been undertaken at the invitation of the governments concerned, and in cooperation with geographers and scientists from those countries.

A new idea in popular exploration is the trend for following in the footsteps of celebrated expeditions of the 19th century. These historic re-creations provide insights to the original expeditions and their difficulties and offer new political and cultural perspectives. Some of the most remarkable explorers, scientists and scholars of the past 175 years have crossed the threshold of the RGS to plan and speak about their travels and their academic research, and to support many other geographical activities. The red building on the corner of Exhibition Road and Kensington Gore continues to occupy a central place on the mental map of anyone with an interest in "that most important and entertaining branch of knowledge, geography".

Vivian Fuchs and Edmund Hillary share a meal en route from the South Pole to the Ross Sea during the Trans-Antarctic Expediton 1955–58.

CHAPTER 3
INTO ALL THE WORLD

INTO ALL THE WORLD

Jonathan Bastable

Previous page: a view of the Karo La Valley, Tibet, taken during the British Mission to the country from 1903–1904 led by Francis Younghusband.

A portrait of Livingstone as the Christian hero: his will is strong, his mind serious, and his eyes can pierce the sinner's soul.

I n our day, it is generally agreed that exploration is a heroic and worthwhile pursuit in itself. We all see that the best possible reason to conquer a mountain is, in George Mallory's dictum, "because it is there". For a modern explorer an uncharted location is like the athlete's finishing line. Get there first, because that is what makes you a winner. But many successful explorers in earlier times had a purpose apart from personal glory. Some of the best-known Victorian travellers were on a mission that, on the face of it at least, had as much to do with the spiritual sphere as the physical globe. Discovery and map-making were secondary to the nobler aim of making the world a better place.

David Livingstone, for example, was first and foremost a missionary. It was through doing the Lord's work, as he saw it, that he became the most famous explorer of his age. He remains almost a patron saint of geographers. His statue stands in a high niche on the wall of the Royal Geographical Society, like a stone apostle on a cathedral façade. But his major discoveries as an explorer proceeded directly from a desire to save African souls. He took a deeply serious and entirely literal view of the Biblical exhortation to "go out into all the world and make disciples". For him, charting the lakes and plateaus of the African interior was the necessary groundwork of Christ's Great Commission. He wrote: "I view the end of the geographical feat as the beginning of the missionary enterprise."

At the same time, Livingstone's missionary enterprise was a broad concept, encompassing such apparently secular activities as international commerce, cultural and political colonization, medical work and philanthropy (in his case, his opposition to the slave trade). These were the reasons he travelled, though it should also be added that he greatly enjoyed the reputation and the material rewards that came his way, and he made sure that he alone got the credit for new discoveries. One could say that all the many motives that might drive exploration were, in some measure, present in Livingstone's life. They form a kind of confluence, much like the mighty river systems of Central Africa that he documented.

Livingstone was God's own explorer, but there were other travellers who tramped this globe with a better world in mind. Among them were Isabella Bird Bishop, a pious spinster who was the outstanding travel writer of her day and the first female Fellow of the Royal Geographical Society; and Francis Younghusband, a soldier in his youth, a mystic in later life, and a man who, as president of the RGS, became the wise Merlin behind the grail quest to reach the summit of Everest.

LIVINGSTONE: THE MAN AND THE MYTHS

One of the most remarkable things about David Livingstone is that he ever managed to emerge from the poverty and hardship of his childhood. He was born in a tenement in Blantyre, near Glasgow, and from the age of 10 he worked as a "piecer" in a cotton mill. A piecer's job was to patrol the clattering machines, crawling beneath them to mend any broken threads. David did this backbreaking work from six in the morning until eight at night. He then went to school for two hours, before returning home to read until his mother begged him to get some sleep, which was usually long after midnight.

Most children in Livingstone's circumstances never managed to learn to read. He not only acquired literacy, but also learned Latin from a primer which he propped on a loom and glanced at as he passed on his endless machine rounds. In the evenings, throughout his adolescence, he studied works of science and travel—and was beaten by his devout father for wasting time on ungodly books. But the young David felt certain that there was no conflict between science and religion, between the God who made the world and the God who revealed Himself through the Bible. In due course he found the perfect way to express this conviction through his life. He would become one of the new brand of practical pastors, a medical missionary.

With his father's grudging consent, and fired by his own relentless will, Livingstone moved to Glasgow to study medicine. After obtaining his qualification, and despite a total lack of a gift for preaching, he was accepted as a field worker by the London Missionary Society. It was then that he made the acquaintance of Robert Moffat, a veteran of African missions. "He asked me whether I thought he would do for Africa," Moffat later wrote. "I believed he would, specifying the vast plains to the north, where I had sometimes seen, in the morning sun, the smoke of a thousand villages where no missionary had ever been." That image of virgin territory—untouched by the word of God or by the sole of a British boot—made up Livingstone's mind. "I will go at once to Africa," he declared.

The tale of David Livingstone's mauling by a lion was depicted time and again by contemporary artists. In this version his "consular cap" lies on the ground just out of reach. It is a kind of symbol of his life, about to be snatched away unless providence intervenes.

Livingstone arrived in Cape Town in March 1841. He made his way north by oxcart to Moffat's mission at Kuruman, 400 miles (640 km) inland. Moffat himself was still in England, and Livingstone soon fell to quarrelling with the older and more experienced missionaries. He felt they lacked his own sense of urgency about saving souls, and he told them so. This was the same single-minded sense of purpose that had propelled him out of the cotton mill, but here it looked like bad temper and impertinence. Within a matter of months Livingstone had decided to found a new mission, where he could build the kingdom of God without having to take account of anyone else's views. "Let us have the spirit of apostle Paul," he said to one young colleague, "not to build on another man's foundations."

From then on Livingstone became a wandering missionary. He worked his way north, and by 1845 he was singlehandedly running a small mission 300 miles (480 km) from the missionary hub of Kuruman. The only European company he had was his new wife Mary, the daughter of his mentor Moffat. She followed him every time he grew restless and moved on to more promising gospel territory. Though she was almost constantly pregnant—having borne three children in as many years—she uncomplainingly endured the heat, the ravaging bouts of malaria, the exhausting journeys and the burdens of motherhood.

Livingstone was finding the work hard too. In four years he made only one convert—a tribal chief named Sechele. But this new Christian soon reverted to his pagan ways, a turn of events that left Livingstone distraught with grief and disappointment. He would have been doubly mortified had he known then that Sechele would remain the only convert of his three decades in Africa. But Livingstone's poor results did not lead him to reassess his low opinion of his fellow workers. And in the days of his fame, he never disabused his public of the assumption that he had been just as successful a preacher

From top to bottom: the sextant that Livingstone carried on his African travels is still in mint condition and in full working order. His collar, on the other hand, is indelibly stained with the grime and sweat of jungle marches. This is the pen he used to record the details of his arduous journeys across the continent.

as he was an explorer. It was always taken for granted that Livingstone was planting new churches wherever he trod. That was part of his myth.

Another element of Livingstone's myth was born during these early years, before he had embarked on his great journeys or made a single significant discovery. In 1845 he was attacked by a lion. It jumped on him and seized him by the left shoulder, shattering his upper arm as it "shook me like a terrier dog does a rat". He would certainly have been killed but for the brave actions of his travelling companions, two of whom were themselves mauled as they shot and speared the lion to death. This incident subsequently acquired an almost Old Testament hue: like Daniel in the lion's den, or Jonah in the belly of the big fish, he was elevated to the status of a prophet—spared by God for a special providence. Not for nothing was the dramatic attack of the lion illustrated in Livingstone's own account of his travels, as well as in countless Sunday-school biographies published down the decades.

But for now Livingstone was a junior worker in the field—one who, in the opinion of his sponsors, spent far too much time on seeking new pastures and not nearly enough tending to the flock he already had. Despite reprimands from London, he continued to make long forays ever deeper into the heart of Africa. In 1849 he accompanied a group of big-game hunters who happened upon Lake Ngami. It had never before been seen by European eyes, so this was Livingstone's first real discovery. He (but not the hunters) received a grant of 25 guineas from the Royal Geographical Society for it. He spent the money on a sextant and other surveying equipment.

These trips were bringing him ever closer to the Zambezi, the great east-west river that was to run like a silver thread through the rest of his life. He saw it for the first time in 1851, during which time the local Africans told him about a great waterfall downstream called Mosi-oa-Tunya, "the smoke that thunders". That was enticing, but for now the river was prize enough. No one had even dreamed of such a waterway in central Africa, but Livingstone understood what it would mean for his work as soon as he set eyes on it. This could be the means to bring Western civilization right to the core of the continent. The Zambezi was surely God's ordained highway. He almost wept as he thought of it.

Livingstone's loyal family came with him on the journey to the Zambezi, and for them it was unspeakably arduous. His babies were a mass of mosquito bites. "I could not touch a square half-inch on the bodies of the children unbitten after a single night's exposure," he wrote. Their mother—pregnant again—was close to physical breakdown, and Mary's frantic parents prevailed on Livingstone to let them return home to Britain to recuperate. He reluctantly agreed to put his family before the gospel for once, and took his wife and children back to Cape Town, where they boarded ship for England. He would not see them again for more than four years.

Livingstone was about to embark on one of the great feats of exploration of the 19th century: a trek on foot and by boat across the width of the African continent. As he made plans, he maintained the belief that he was a kind of prospector for God. He would go looking for sites where missions could be set up like evangelical lighthouses in the benighted interior of Africa. He felt that these sites would also serve as centres for wholesome European trade, which would undermine the dreadful traffic in slaves that was the main commercial activity in central Africa at the time. Moreover, an influx of British goods would, he felt sure, help to promote a civilized Western outlook, so rendering the Africans more open to the message of the gospel. For this strategy he adopted the slogan "Commerce and Christianity", and neither Livingstone nor his contemporaries saw any contradiction between the two. The phrase makes it clear that he was happy to blaze a trail for merchants as well as for missionaries. He was determined to save Africans from slavery, damnation—or both.

Livingstone set off from the Cape in June 1852. His plan was to travel north to the Zambezi, then to turn west and head for the Atlantic coast. After that he would retrace his steps to the interior and then strike out east, following the unexplored central reaches of the Zambezi all the way to the Indian Ocean. In this way he would describe a great letter T, 1,500 miles (2,400 km) tall and 2,400 miles (3,900 km) wide, on the inverted parabola of sub-Saharan Africa. He would also, he hoped, show that the Zambezi was a navigable carriageway for ships, with all the benefits—material and spiritual—that they could bring to the African heartland.

It took Livingstone a year to reach the Barotse Valley, the junction of his notional letter T, and the place where he hoped to find a suitable site for a trading post cum mission station. Even this first and relatively easy stage of his journey was nightmarishly difficult. He was racked with fever all the way, and when he passed his old home north of Kuruman he found it had been vandalized and pillaged by Boer militants. But far worse, from Livingstone's point of view, was his failure to find any spot that was not infested by both

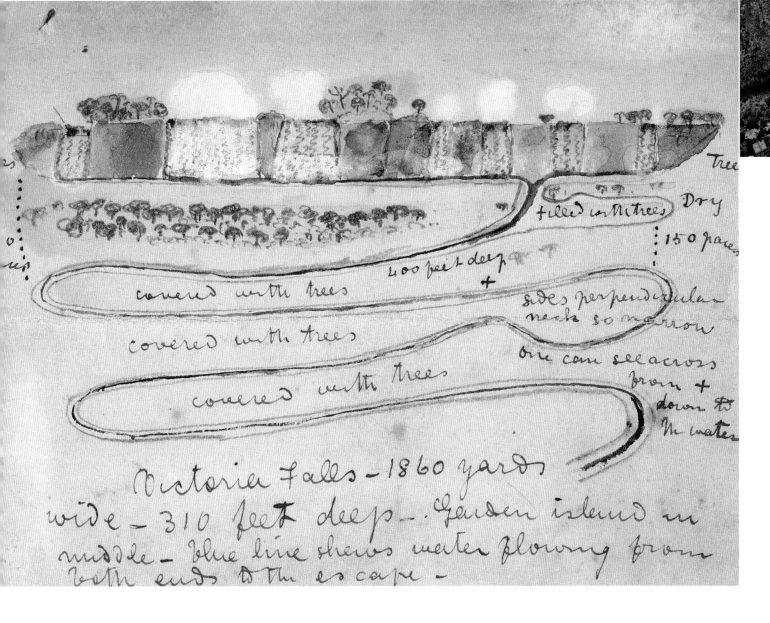

It was probably on his second visit in 1860 that Livingstone made this annotated sketch (left) of the switchback course of the Zambezi as it approaches Victoria Falls. An aerial photograph, above, reveals at a glance the terrain that Livingstone laboriously crossed on foot.
Photo: Martha Holmes

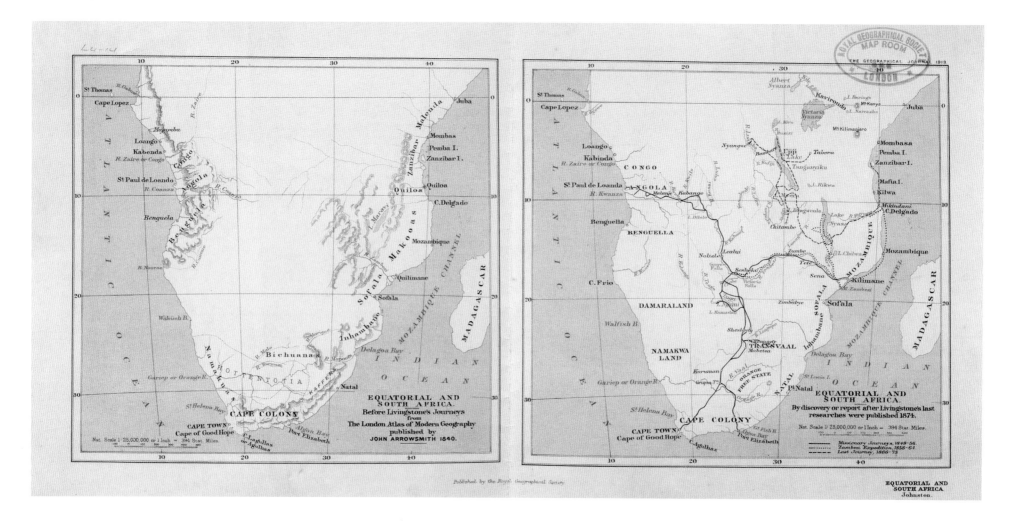

Livingstone's greatest achievement as a geographer was to fill in many of the blanks on the map of central Africa. The great network of rivers, which are the main feature of the region, were undreamed of until he mapped their twists and turns.

mosquitos and slave traders. The Barotse Valley would not do, and when Livingstone turned left and headed for the west coast he was sickened as much by a sense of defeat as by the effects of malaria.

He arrived in the Angolan port of Luanda in April 1854. He was already famous, news of his journey having preceded him, but he was also three-quarters dead. He could barely move or even hold a pen for three months. He could have abandoned his quest now and sailed home to a sympathetic welcome, but the knowledge of his failure combined with his own rock-like will prevented him from taking this easy way out. As soon as he had recovered his strength he set out back east—to cross his T and in so doing find a trade route to the far side of Africa.

This third leg of Livingstone's journey took the better part of another year, during which time he made his way to the point where he had heard tell of the "smoke that thunders" five years previously. Now he headed downstream and saw the great cascade for the first time. He gave it an English name in honor of his queen—Victoria Falls. But beyond the Falls, north of the river, he found an even greater treasure: a high plateau called Bakota, a cool and mosquito-free place that could serve as the foundation of his missionary colony.

It remained only to show that the river was navigable from here to the east coast. But now Livingstone the geographer made the biggest mistake of his life. Crossing to the south bank, he left the river to make an overland detour, and so missed the Kebra Basa Rapids. Had he seen them he would have known at once that the cataracts rendered the Zambezi completely impassable to shipping: Bakota was cut off by the Victoria Falls on one side and by the rapids on the other.

This on its own would have been no more than a stroke of bad luck. But, unaccountably, Livingstone failed to take altitude readings before he left the river or when he rejoined it. Had he done so, he would have realized that there must be a steep descent somewhere in-between. He was even told about Kebra Basa, but in his unbridled enthusiasm managed to convince himself that it amounted to no more than a few large rocks in the stream. By the time he arrived at the Portuguese-administered port of Quelimane, in May 1856, he firmly believed that he had successfully mapped out a route to the promised upland.

Livingstone's great African odyssey was at an end. He had made the first documented crossing of the continent, and was ready to sail home in a British warship. Within days of his arrival in Britain he attended the Royal Geographical Society to receive its gold medal, and Roderick Murchison, president of the Society, orchestrated much of the rapturous publicity that now engulfed him. Livingstone, a pioneer of the unknown, was greeted with the same wonderment and admiration that more than a century later was accorded to lunar astronauts. He was the Neil Armstrong of his day. He dined out, sometimes even drinking champagne despite his teetotal principles. He was invited to tea with Queen Victoria and Prince Albert. He embarked on lecture tours, always wearing the battered "consular cap" that now became his trademark. He also wrote a book, which was favourably reviewed by Charles Dickens, and which earned him a fortune in royalties. The Victorian public was astonished to learn from it that Africa contained wide rivers, boundless lakes, dense green jungles and endless grassy steppes. Before Livingstone, most people believed all Africa was a vast desert wasteland.

While in England, Livingstone quietly resigned from his missionary society. With Murchison acting as an intermediary, he took a government appointment as British consul to Quelimane. He was granted a handsome salary, and charged with leading an expedition to explore the Zambezi more fully. Now a "private Christian", Livingstone hoped to use his new secular authority as a representative of the British crown to drive the slave traders out of Portuguese East Africa.

The Zambezi expedition was a very different undertaking from his trans-African journey. He was no longer the lone European, answerable only to himself. He was now the leader of a team of explorers. Among them were his brother Charles, a pastor; Thomas Baines, an artist and an experienced traveller in his own right; and Norman Bedingfield, a naval captain. There was also a mining geologist, a botanist and a ship's engineer. The British government provided the expedition with a steamer, *The Pearl*, which it was hoped would carry them first to Africa, then far inland along the broad tracts of the Zambezi. Livingstone also took an 80-foot (24-m) launch in kit form. It was christened the *Ma Robert*, the native name for his wife.

Mary Livingstone herself was to accompany her husband on the journey. But on the first leg of the voyage to Africa, she became sick. It soon became clear that she was pregnant once again. This was a personal disaster for her, given the dreadful toll that previous pregnancies had taken on her health, and it was the first of the many misfortunes that were to befall the group. She left the ship in Cape Town, and went to the relative comfort of her parents' mission at Kuruman.

Meanwhile, Livingstone and his crew proceeded round the Cape to the mouth of the Zambezi on Africa's east coast. The river's delta proved to be shallow and completely clogged with mangrove swamps. There was no hope of taking a ship as large as *The Pearl* upriver, or any distance inland at all. There was nothing for it but to bolt together the *Ma Robert* and proceed in the much smaller craft. It was at this point that serious discord began to break out. Bedingfield took deep umbrage at finding himself captain

The frontispiece of this popular biography of Livingstone, published shortly after his death, looks almost like a coat of arms. Above the image of the good doctor is an African slave, his chains broken at last; below him is his Bible.

of a mere leaky riverboat rather than a naval steamer. He also objected to Livingstone's constant meddling in the workaday business of sailing it.

Bedingfield's truculence turned almost to mutiny when the route upriver took the party into the midst of a small war between the Portuguese and the native tribes. He came close to abandoning Livingstone ashore and taking the boat out of the war zone. And whenever he raised reasonable objections to Livingstone's plans, the saintly doctor responded with lordly condescension or downright sarcasm. Finally, the sea captain resigned and returned home, leaving Livingstone to navigate his own boat to Bakota. "Bedingfield turned out to be an unmitigated muff," Livingstone later wrote. "I never met such a fool and a liar."

But Livingstone looked the fool himself, and all the optimistic declarations he had made in London were proved untrue, when the boat at last reached the foot of the impassable Kebra Basa Rapids. This was the mighty obstacle that he had chosen to write off as negligible despite having never seen it—almost as if he could, by the force of his will, bend the very geography of Africa to his grand design. Now that he was up against the cataract Livingstone, like Quixote tilting at windmills, drove the *Ma Robert* on until he crashed its bow against the high pillars of rock. When he turned back downstream, he knew that his entire vision of a Christian commonwealth in Bakotaland lay in ruins.

Livingstone's crew was also in a state of disintegration. Bad feeling was rife, and Livingstone was too self-absorbed and aloof to deal with it. The source of most of the trouble was Charles Livingstone, who possessed all of his older brother's

Thomas Baines's artistic record of the Zambezi expedition is one of the great treasures of the RGS archive. In this watercolour the artist places himself at the centre, while the troublesome would-be photographer Charles Livingstone is reduced to an ant-like speck in the bottom right-hand corner.

Baobab trees, looking like grotesquely gnarled hands, could not help but catch the artist's eye. Livingstone's wife Mary was buried under such a tree in 1862.

Livingstone's party had no qualms about shooting wildlife for fun. This painting by Baines depicts an incident that occurred on the River Shire in 1859. Baines was not there, but drew the scene from accounts given to him by members of the ship's crew.

faults but none of his redeeming features. He also had faults all of his own: he was idle, scheming and a gossip-monger—and he took a violent dislike to the artist Thomas Baines. The animosity was partly due to the fact that Charles considered himself a photographer (though he had no real talent for the new technology) and saw no need for anything as old-hat and impractical as a painter on the expedition.

Charles used his position as his brother's assistant to whisper against Baines. He accused him of painting unofficial subjects on expedition time, and even trumped up an accusation of pilfering from the ship's stores. This was too much for the talented Baines, who subsequently handed in his notice (after which he was forbidden to eat at the table with the others). The wonderfully vivid sketches and watercolours he made in Africa are among the greatest treasures of the Royal Geographical Society's archive. But for the pettiness of Charles Livingstone, there might have been many more.

Mary Livingstone rejoined her husband on the Zambezi a month after the crushing disappointment of Kebra Basa. She had seen little of her husband during the past decade, and these lonely years had taken their toll. She was bitter and angry with him for leaving her to bring up the children alone—and she told him so. Livingstone discovered to his horror that she had taken to drink to help ease her misery. This unhappy time constituted their last weeks together. In April 1862 she died of malaria. He buried her under a baobab tree, wept like a child over her grave, then reboarded the boat that was named after her and resumed the expedition.

Livingstone now conceived a new scheme to save his expedition from total failure. Years before he had heard tell of a huge lake at the head of the River Shire, a tributary that joined the Zambezi back the way they had come. Perhaps the shores of the lake would be God's intended site for his mission—and if not, he could at least claim the lake as a bona fide discovery. So the *Ma Robert* turned its prow back to the east, then headed north up the River Shire. In November 1863 the boat arrived at Nyasa—meaning the "lake of stars". The reality was far less romantic than the name. It turned out that the southern shores of the lake were an established staging post for Arab slave traders taking their wares to market in Zanzibar. As such, it would not do for Livingstone's "Commerce and Christianity" project: no legitimate traders would ever want to come here, and it would be impossible to plant a free community of African cotton-growers in this place.

The British government now cut its losses and recalled the expedition. Livingstone arrived home in 1864. He had amassed a great deal of information, but had not fulfilled the aims of his mission. *The Times* printed a withering attack on the whole undertaking: "We were promised cotton, sugar and indigo and of course we get none. We were promised trade; and there is no trade.

An extract, below, from the RGS committee minutes to David Livingstone prior to his East African trip describing what readings he should undertake on his journey. The minutes, held in the Society's archive, are dated 27 June 1865.

These slave chains, right, are part of a set brought back by David Livingstone. They consist of neck-irons complete with loops through which a fourteen foot chain would have been threaded.

We were promised converts to the Gospel, and not one has been made." It was all a far cry from the adulation of his previous return to Britain.

But Livingstone still had friends, in particular Roderick Murchison of the Royal Geographical Society. In 1865, the Society commissioned Livingstone to go back to Africa and solve the longstanding mystery of the source of the Nile. This time, wrote Murchison, he would be "unshackled by other avocations than those of the geographical explorer". Livingstone took the job, hoping once again to use it for his own moral ends. He wanted to expose the extent of the Arab slave trade north of Portuguese-held territory.

Livingstone left Britain for the last time in August 1865, landing in East Africa in March 1866. With a small team of Africans (after his past experience he did not want to travel with Europeans again) he marched inland to Lake Nyasa, then headed north to explore the lake system that centred on the long serpentine form of Lake Tanganyika, one possible source of the Nile. Once again the expedition got off to a bad start. Many of the supposedly loyal Africans deserted him, and the country was racked by conflict. A year after heading inland he had made no significant discoveries. Some of the deserters had even made it back to the coast and announced that he was dead. This news was greeted with a fair amount of scepticism, but some newspapers in England printed Livingstone's obituary nevertheless.

Livingstone himself knew nothing of this. For four years he trekked around the central African watershed with a few faithful followers. He was making notes, following wild hunches about the Nile, increasingly relying on the kindness and cooperation of the Arabs whose trade he despised. His health was failing him. Fever and internal bleeding meant that he was laid up for weeks or months at a time. In 1871 he came to rest in the slave town of Ujiji, on the shores of Lake Tanganyika. His supplies had all been used or stolen, and he was bitterly contemplating the humiliation of asking the slavers for a loan. At this low point in Livingstone's fortune a genuine miracle happened. On one morning in the autumn of 1871, a white man strode into Ujiji preceded by an African carrying an American flag. This astonishing apparition, like an angel in a pith helmet, marched up to the stooping old gentleman, doffed his hat, and said: "Doctor Livingstone, I presume".

Henry Morton Stanley was a journalist with the *New York Herald*, and he had just achieved the greatest scoop of his career—perhaps of the entire 19th century. Many expeditions had been sent out to find Livingstone, some of them sponsored by the Royal Geographical Society, but Stanley got there first. It has been said that the handshake at Ujiji marks the moment when getting there first became the primary goal of exploration. Certainly it mattered very much to the next generation of explorers—cold-weather men such as Robert Falcon Scott and Ernest Shackleton. At any rate, Livingstone the explorer had himself now been discovered. It was as if, over the decades, he had become an immovable geographical feature of the African continent.

Stanley spent several months with Livingstone, travelling around with him and helping to restore him to health. Then he headed back to England in triumph. Stanley wrote a book about his experience with the tabloid-style title *How I Found Livingstone*. It made a celebrity of the author, and restored the somewhat battered reputation of its subject. Livingstone was no longer the irascible and rather unlikeable failure of the Zambezi expedition; now and for ever after he was the almost Christ-like apostle of the "dark continent" (Stanley's coinage), the friend of the African, and the scourge of the slave trade.

Henry Morton Stanley was told by the proprietor of the New York Herald *that he could spend as much money as it might take to find Livingstone. Stanley kitted out his expedition in Zanzibar, where he hired 2,000 African porters for the journey into the interior.*

The RGS archive contains both David Livingstone's cap and Henry Stanley's pith helmet, the very items they were wearing when they met at Ujiji in November 1871. The distinctive cap was a key element of Livingstone's public image, and he had several identical specimens made for him by the firm of Starkey's in Bond Street.

Stanley had urged Livingstone to come home with him, but the old man refused. Possibly he sensed that if he left now he would inevitably be paraded like an elephant, and that he would become Stanley's trophy. He preferred to stay and try to solve the riddle of the source of the Nile, then perhaps return with a triumph of his own. But it was not to be. On the morning of May 1, 1873, one of his African followers found Livingstone dead. His emaciated body was kneeling beside his bed in an attitude of prayer.

Like Moses with the promised land of Canaan, Livingstone died before he reached his goal. But he did get home. His followers dried his corpse in the sun, having first removed his heart and buried it in African soil. Then they wrapped him in calico and carried him the 1,000 miles (1,600 km) to the coast—a journey that took nearly a year. From here the explorer's body was shipped to England, where it was identified at postmortem by the toothmarks of the lion on the broken bones of his left arm.

Livingstone's desiccated body lay in state at the Royal Geographical Society, and was buried at Westminster Abbey on April 18, 1874. Henry Stanley was one of the pallbearers. In June 1873, barely a month after his death, the British government forced the closure of the slave market in Zanzibar, effectively ending the traffic in human property in East Africa. Livingstone had been working for this throughout his entire life. For all his towering accomplishments as a geographer, it would have been his proudest day.

James Chuma and Abdullah Susi, the two followers of Livingstone who escorted his body back home, also brought his many manuscripts. Here they pose with some of the explorer's relatives as they inspect the papers. The lion skin is the photographer's heavy-handed reminder that we are dealing with an African subject.

THE BIRD UNCAGED

The peregrinations of David Livingstone were surely a subject of close interest to the young Isabella Bird. Her father, the Reverend Edward Bird, was a cousin of the great antislavery campaigner William Wilberforce—so Isabella had the abolitionist cause in her blood. She was also interested in travel—in her early 20s she published an anonymous little book about a trip she made to New York. Isabella and her sister Henrietta were both stoutly practical Christians. They lived a life of bourgeois Victorian philanthropy, devoting much of their time to those who were sick or unfortunate.

Isabella Bird Bishop took to travel late in life. Her vividly written books, full of insight and incident, were bestsellers in their day.

Not that Isabella was free from sickness or misfortune herself. As a child she suffered dreadfully with spinal disease, and had a large tumor removed from her back when she was 18. Pain kept her confined to bed for long periods, and severely limited the time she could spend on her favourite recreation: horseriding. When their parents died, the earnest Bird sisters—then in their late 20s—moved to a genteel house in Edinburgh. Isabella seemed set for the life of the professional invalid: reading, rest cures and good works when her frail constitution allowed it. No one could have guessed that her true life had yet to begin, that she was to become one of the most intrepid and wide-ranging travellers of her age.

Curiously, the ill health that had blighted Isabella's youth made a traveller of her in middle-age. Her doctors, in desperation, prescribed sea air, so she went on a cruise to New York—but returned sicker than when she had left. In 1872, by now 40 years old, she tried again. This time she booked a passage on a ship to Australia, half-convinced it would finish her off altogether. In fact, it made her into a new person.

The metamorphosis of Miss Bird occurred en route to Hawaii, then known as the Sandwich Isles. Having taken a deep and irrational dislike to Australia, she was so desperate to escape that she caught a leaky rat-infested paddle-steamer heading for the United States via the islands. The squalor of the ship, and the real danger that it might sink, cheered Miss Bird immensely. Her impressive range of ailments all evaporated. By the time the ship put in at Hawaii she was full of strength, bursting with energy and ready to explore. It was as if boredom were her only disease and excitement the obvious cure.

This erstwhile invalid even climbed Mauna Loa, the largest volcano in the world. She wrote an ecstatic note to Henrietta from the lip of its crater: "... red and glorious burned and glowed the splendour of the fire fountain. Oh light that never was on sea or shore! Light at once of beauty and terror. Fires appeared all round the edge, and here and there all over the expanse lone stars of fire kept bursting out, showing that underneath that black crust was a liquid sea of living fire ..." This letter, like all her subsequent letters, contains the kind of vivid descriptions and tells the engaging stories that would later make her famous. Her books were no more or less than an edited version of her letters home.

Bird spent seven months on the island Eden of Hawaii. She noted that the people of the islands were trusting, hospitable and curious. Their lives were easy and, like the inhabitants of the original Eden, they were unaware of such dour concepts as sin: they were happily idle, joyfully and carelessly promiscuous. The old stay-at-home Miss Bird of Edinburgh could not but disapprove of the

The town elders of the city of Seoul gathered in ceremonial garb to greet Mrs Bird Bishop on her visit to Korea in 1895.

Isabella Bird Bishop was fascinated by the architecture of the East. Many of her photographs are studies of buildings (opposite page and below).

Hawaiian peoples' unbuttoned ways (and there were plenty of American missionaries on the islands trying as hard as any Livingstone to reform them), but somehow the new, itinerant Isabella found it all utterly charming.

Her enjoyment was enhanced when she found that she could ride without pain if she sat astride her horse cowboy-style, rather than persist in the ladylike practice of riding side-saddle. This was a symbolic discovery. Henceforth in all her travels Isabella was happiest when she was far from Western influences and Western people—from anyone, in fact, who would tut-tut at a lady sitting full-square on her mount. From now on she chose the path less trodden, and was saddened when she encountered what she termed "grooviness"—the tendency of people and places to be predictable or remain stuck in a rut.

The mere threat of boredom was enough to make her feel physically ill. She needed new experiences to stay well, and also to have something to write about. Though later trips were taken with some philanthropic purpose in mind, the fact is that Bird wanted to tell the public—and, in the first instance, her sister Hennie—what she thought of the great gaudy world out there. She was not an explorer as such, because she was not drawn to empty, uncharted places. But she was a born travel writer, and she needed above all to meet interesting people.

Miss Bird had perhaps the most engaging encounter of her life on the next stage of her journey. She sailed on to mainland America and headed for Colorado, then still very much a rowdy tract of the Wild West. High in the mountains she met a trapper named Rocky Mountain Jim. He was shaggy, untamed and he had recently had one eye clawed out by a bear. The effect of this was that he looked extremely handsome from one side, and rather ghastly from the other. This was a fair reflection of his character. He was a man given to extremes. He could be charming, intelligent, poetic and courteous; or he could be uncouth, voluble and filled with drunken self-loathing and remorse.

Jim was, in a word, completely fascinating. The English spinster and the American frontiersman fell totally in love with each other, and conducted a passionate albeit entirely chaste affair. But they both knew that their worlds were too different for them ever to be together in the long term. Isabella left for England, and Mountain Jim was killed in a bar fight a few months later. His epitaph was the affectionate account of him that Isabella gave in her book *A Lady's Life in the Rocky Mountains*. She was immensely relieved on publication that "the critics have not scented out impropriety"—but by that time she was in any case away on new adventures.

She went first to Japan, then to Malaya—and produced a book about each destination. She would doubtless have stayed on the road had not personal problems intervened. In 1880 her sister fell ill and died. Isabella was devastated. She stopped travelling and stopped writing—who would she be writing for now? In the depths of mourning she accepted an offer of marriage from Dr. John Bishop, a friend of the family who had nursed Henrietta through her last illness. They lived quietly in England and the south of France. But Dr. Bishop too was a sick man: he died in 1886, in the fifth year of their marriage.

In Japan and China, Mrs Bishop was drawn to Buddhist temples (above) and graveyards (right). But the Christian lady found the liturgy of Buddhism utterly depressing: "… dull gleams of dead gold … the low boom of a temple drum … the sound of litanies wafted on a wailing breeze … I felt as if I were far from the haunts of living men."

Isabella, now 60 years old, assuaged her grief in the same way that years before she had eased her physical sickness: by going overseas. This time her trips had a more soulful purpose. She went to Tibet and India to endow hospitals in the names of her sister and her husband. She travelled through the Middle East, visiting the last adherents of the ancient Nestorian sect of Christians, who were then being persecuted by the Kurds. On her return she spoke to a Commons select committee on their plight, and embarked on a lecture tour of missionary societies (she addressed many of the same institutions that had played host to Livingstone a generation before). She also took the time to learn the basics of the relatively new art of photography.

At this time, the Royal Geographical Society was involved in a heated debate over the admission of women. Bird fanned the flames by saying that the bar was a "dastardly injustice to women". When at last 14 "well-qualified ladies" were grudgingly admitted, she was among their number. She later became the first woman to give a paper at the Society. It is as a result of the belated admission of women that the RGS now has the photographs of Bird's last great long journey. The images document Korea, China and Japan during the period when these ancient civilizations were vying against each other, and at the same time coping with a rising tide of Western influence.

Her swan song as a traveller was a trip to Morocco, which she undertook at the age of 70. She returned to England —that "dim, pale island", as she called it—and was in the midst of planning a further trip to China when she died, at home in her bed, in 1904.

Most of Mrs Bishop's later travels were undertaken with philanthropy in mind. She wanted to do good while she was abroad. These solemn children were photographed by her at their orphanage in the Japanese town of Gifu.

Boats such as the one below would shoot the rapids on the Yangtse River. Mrs Bishop wrote that each boat carried "a curious functionary—a man carrying a white flag on which was written 'Powers of the water, give a luck star for the journey …'"

This was not the only angry face that Mrs Bishop encountered in China. In the provincial city of Liang-Shan Hsien she was almost lynched by a xenophobic mob. They attacked her party, yelling that the "foreign devil" ate children.

A COLONEL'S ROAD TO ENLIGHTENMENT

At the time of Isabella Bird Bishop's death, an armed British column was marching into Tibet to take control of the capital, the holy city of Lhasa. This attacking force was under the command of Colonel Francis Younghusband. He was one of that determined and energetic breed of Anglo-Indian officer who managed to successfully combine the job of soldiering with the business of exploration.

Younghusband had earned his explorer's spurs in 1887 when, as a lieutenant in the King's Dragoon Guards, he had trekked from Beijing (Peking) across the Gobi Desert, through Turkestan and over the high Himalayas into Kashmir. It was a fantastical journey, as he himself later wrote: "Since the time of Marco Polo, six centuries before, no European had travelled from China to Central Asia." It was also a remarkably bold undertaking for Younghusband personally: "Nowhere in Peking had we been able to obtain information about the road across the desert. I had never been in a desert, and here we were a thousand miles or so of one to be crossed. At the back of all, the Himalayas, to cross which had previously been considered a journey in itself."

The mountains made a deep impression on the youthful Younghusband. To his philosophical cast of mind, the unexplored peaks were a metaphor for the human longing for higher things. But more than that, the very act of mountaineering seemed to him a kind of moral endeavour. By climbing ever higher, one might also explore the unknown cols and crevasses of one's own soul.

In 1888, when Lieutenant Younghusband arrived back at his post in India, his fellow officers greeted him with awe and respect. He was immediately sent to England to give an account of his experiences, both to his superiors and to the Royal Geographical Society. The RGS elected him a Fellow at 24 years old, and he thereby became the youngest member of the Society.

Throughout the 1890s, Younghusband prowled the borderlands of the British Empire like a lone wolf. He worked as a political agent in various posts and wrote for newspapers. But much of his time was spent thinking about religion, and investigating the similarities between Christ and Buddha. At the same time he was a devoted admirer of Charles Darwin and his evolutionary theories, which he applied to his own philosophical quest. He conceived an idea of a future in which humanity might evolve a universal form of belief in which the divine would be as grand and visible as a Himalayan peak on a cloudless day.

In 1903, when Younghusband was serving as British resident in Indore, Lord Curzon appointed him to lead the military expedition into Tibet. From a political point of view, Younghusband's Tibetan operation was disastrous. His troops massacred 700 Tibetans en route, and he far exceeded his remit by occupying the holy city of Lhasa and imposing a treaty on the Tibetan authorities. For this he received a reprimand from the British government. But for Younghusband personally, Tibet was a life-changing experience. On his departure from the country he had a kind of epiphany—a moment of almost pure Buddhist enlightenment. "I went off alone to the mountain-side," he wrote. "The

The Potala Palace, opposite, residence of the Dalai Lama, is perched on a mountain top high above the Lhasa Valley. This is the view that Francis Younghusband had as he approached along the ridge.

unclouded sky was of the clearest Tibetan blue. The mountains were bathed in purply haze. I was beside myself with untellable joy. The whole world was ablaze with the same ineffable bliss that was burning within me. I felt in touch with the flaming heart of the world. I was boiling over with love for the whole world, and henceforth life for me was naught but buoyancy and light."

He spent the rest of his life exploring this experience—through his writing on mystical themes, and through his geographical work. When he became president of the RGS in 1919, he expounded upon his outdoor brand of mysticism in an address entitled "Natural Beauty and Geographical Science". The great symbol of his world-view was Everest itself, "poised high in heaven as the spotless pinnacle of the world". Though his own exploring days were over, he used his presidency to promote several expeditions, including Mallory's, to the greatest mountain of all. He saw the successive attempts to climb Everest as a kind of battle for perfection of the human spirit, and the mountaineers themselves as something akin to warrior-monks on their way to a lofty nirvana.

Characteristically, Younghusband was adamant that the climbers should not use oxygen canisters to ascend the summit—that to do so would somehow cheapen the achievement: "A branch of science might have won a success," he said, "but man would have lost a chance of knowing himself." He was naturally devastated when, in 1924, Mallory and Irvine died in the attempt to conquer Everest, and he did not live to see Edmund Hillary's successful ascent in 1953. Perhaps he would have been strangely disappointed if he had: for what then would there be left to strive for?

Both David Livingstone and Isabella Bird would have agreed with Younghusband that exploration properly entails going beyond oneself, that the travail of travel has a spiritual dimension. But the experiences of these three voyagers were widely divergent. Bird was transformed by travel; it restored her soul and made her physically strong. David Livingstone, on the other hand, slowly destroyed his body through travelling, but the core of the man—the essential granite of his personality and his convictions—changed not one jot throughout his life: it only grew harder and more impermeable. Francis Younghusband was different again. His career as an explorer was a process of continual inner change. His travels were a lifelong pilgrimage into the mystical heart of things, and for all the thousands of miles he trekked or all the mountain passes he traversed, he was always on the same Damascus road.

A photographic album of Younghusband's exploits is held in the Society's archive. Here, "the British flag [is] hoisted in Tibet proper for the first time Jan. 1904."

This highly decorative mandala or "wheel of life" was photographed by a member of Younghusband's Tibet expedition. In Tibetan thought the mandala is a kind of icon, but it is also a power object, a focus for prayerful meditation.

Colonel Younghusband's column had several bloody encounters with the Tibetan army on the way into Lhasa, above. On each occasion the defenders were decimated. In July 1904 a force of Gurkhas defeated a Tibetan army at Karo La; at the time no battle had ever been fought at such a high altitude.

The great fortress city of Gyantse Jong (above and left) was occupied by the British in July 1904. Younghusband was supposed to have stopped here, but he pushed on to Lhasa—only to find that the young Dalai Lama had already fled.

GALLERY

A MIRROR OF LIFE

Previous pages: George Lowe, a member of the 1953 Mount Everest Expedition, in front of a mani wall, carved and painted with prayers, in Nepal.
Photo: Alfred Gregory/RGS

The indigenous population of Papua New Guinea is one of the most diverse in the world. Many tribes are isolated from each other by the mountainous terrain. The result is a riot of mini-cultures that goes far beyond the variety of colourful body decorations. Many of the 650 languages spoken by tribal peoples are totally unrelated. And until recently some tribes were unaware of the existence of neighbours just a few miles away.
Photos: Edward Mendell

A Sinalaco woman sifting quinoa
on the banks of the Salar de Uyuni
in Bolivia. Quinoa is a cereal that
can be dried like cornflakes or boiled
like rice. It has been a staple food
in South America for millennia.
Photo: Eric Lawrie

Harry Philby photographed these Jewish merchants at a Saudi market in 1936. In Islam Jews are seen as dhimmi, "protected peoples". But most Saudi Jews left the country after the Second World War.
Photo: Harry St John Philby/RGS

Climbing and messing about in the water are boyish pursuits the world over. This youth, left, is clambering up the ruined columns of the ancient city of Marib in Yemen. The young canoeist, right, is a member of the Digo, the largest ethnic group in the region of Msambweni, Kenya.
Photos: Chris Bradley (left) and Robert Maletta (right)

Overleaf, bathing in the waters of the River Ganges at Benares, northern India, in 1925. Benares, now known as Varanasi, is one of the holiest cities in India. The waterfront is made up of long flights of stone steps called ghats (meaning "landings"). The city and the river are sacred to Hindus, who believe that those who die and are cremated on the waterfront are released from the cycle of reincarnation and go straight to heaven.
Photo: RGS

In the village of Cocuy, high in the Andean uplands of Colombia, a trader rests after a day at market. In this rural part of the country, a broadbrimmed hat and poncho are standard dress for men and women.
Photo: Eric Lawrie

Atop the peak of Jabbaren in Algeria's Tassili n'Ajjer mountain range, a Touareg guide sits and surveys the lumpy plateau below. The mountain range is composed largely of sandstone. In many places there are ancient cave paintings depicting mysterious bubble-headed human figures.
Photo: Chris Bradley

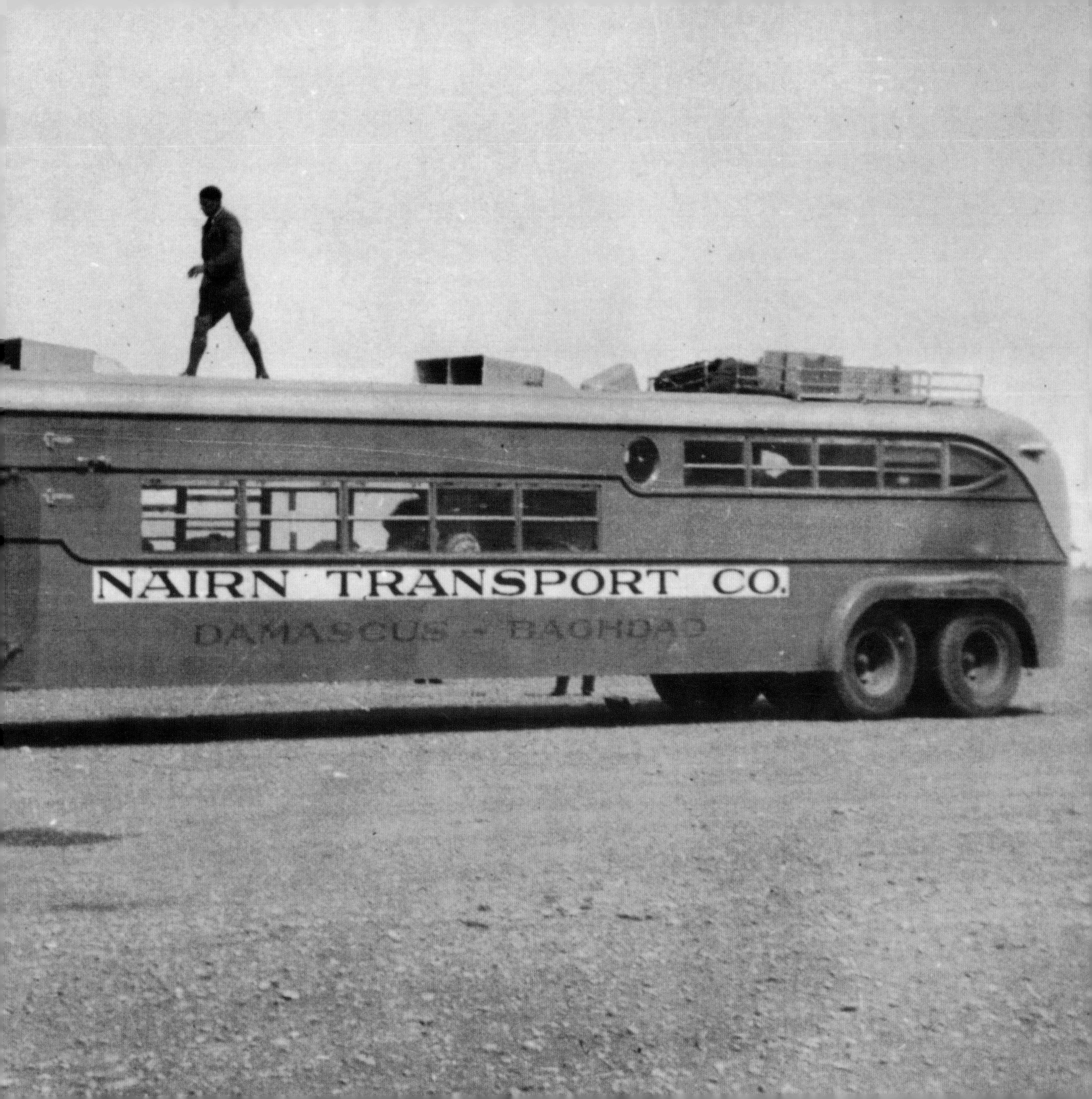
NAIRN TRANSPORT CO.
DAMASCUS – BAGHDAD

Two Touareg guides stand in a sand sea near Djanet, Algeria. The Touareg people are descended from the Berbers of North Africa. Their characteristic headdress is called the "tagelmust", and is usually (but not here) a deep-blue colour. Some Touareg continue to live a nomadic way of life as cattle-breeders, but many are now settled.
Photo: Chris Bradley

Women winnowing rice in
Thaivur, India. In this image,
the energetic process of separating
the chaff from grain looks like
a graceful form of dance.
Photo: Michael Freeman

Lalibela is one of Ethiopia's holiest sites. It is a complex of Coptic churches carved from the rock on a high plateau. Some of them—like St. George's, right—are hidden in deep gullies. Coptic Christianity, said to have been founded by the apostle Mark in the first century, has 30 million adherents in Ethiopia. Below, a Coptic hermit keeps vigil in one of Lalibela's cell-like caves. Photos: Chris Bradley (above) and Sybil Sassoon (right)

A priest holds aloft a cross during a religious procession in Ethiopia. It is widely believed that the Ark of the Covenant, which disappeared after the Babylonians destroyed the Temple in Jerusalem, remains in the safekeeping of the Ethiopian Orthodox priesthood at Axum.
Photo: Robert Maletta

The monolith at Axum, northern Ethiopia is more than 2,000 years old and measures 75 feet (23 m) in height. The city, located at the base of the Adoua mountains, was the centre of the Axumite Kingdom, which emerged around the time of the birth of Jesus and declined in the 12th century.
Photo: John Miles

Bhutan is a tiny mountain kingdom set in the upper reaches of the Himalayas. Outside influence is resisted as a matter of government policy, and travel by foreigners is restricted. So this striking portrait of a highland villager, much in the tradition of Frank Kingdon-Ward's ethnographic studies, is a rarity.
Photo: Bruce Herrod

The bowler hat immediately marks out this woman as a Bolivian. The colourful shawl is also typical, and is usually worn with a full skirt called a "pollera". This form of dress, which is European in origin, was imposed by the Spanish colonialists to discourage indigenous Indian dress. But over the decades this alien outfit has come to be seen as the authentic badge of Bolivian cultural independence.
Photo: Julia Ling

This abandoned truck at the village of Barentu Kunama in Eritrea has been stripped of all useful parts and left to rust. It is both a relic and a symbol of the conflict with Ethiopia.
Photo: John Miles

A woman of the Dinka tribe stands in the ruins of the village of Maper in southern Sudan. The Dinka people were subject to terrifying attacks during Sudan's bloody civil war. Raiders from the north of the country would sweep into a village, murder the men, and take the women and children into slavery.
Photo: John Miles

Overleaf, a crowd gathers for market in Mali. Most of the population of this landlocked West African country is concentrated in the fertile southern half of the country, where the cotton fields are watered by the River Niger. The northern half of Mali consists mostly of desert, and is inhabited by Touareg tribesmen.
Photo: Chris Caldicott

A gilded pavilion within the Potala Palace in Lhasa, Tibet. The Potala is the former residence of the Dalai Lama, who is now in exile. Opposite, curious children inside the more humble surroundings of their school in Thimi, west of the city of Bhaktapur, in Nepal.

Photos: Chris Bradley (right) and John R. Jones (opposite page)

*A camera does not merely record
a scene; sometimes it creates the
photographic moment. Both these
pictures were taken in a remote part
of western Nepal, and they tell
a story about the human fascination
with the outlandish and the exotic
—in this case the alien presence
of the photographer himself.*
Photos: Steve Razzetti

These hills in Nepal have been terraced to make them suitable for farming. As a result they look like a manmade city of broad steps and ziggurats which makes for an amazing view.
Photo: David Constantine

Isabella Bird Bishop took these two pictures during her visit to China in 1895; a musician, left, and two bottle sellers, opposite, with their wares in the court of Sivaton Hospital.
Photos: Isabella Bird Bishop/RGS

Overleaf, flooded rice fields in the Kullu district of Himachal Pradesh, northern India. The inundated fields are a shallow sea of green. The floodwater not only irrigates the land for the rice, but also serves to keep down the many weeds which flourish in drier soil.
Photo: Nick Eakins

A farmer ploughs his paddy field in Klaten, a farming region of Java, Indonesia. But for the fact that it is in colour, this picture could have been taken any time in the past century or more. The oxen, the plough and the nature of the task are as timeless as the seasons.
Photo: Adrian Arbib

Above, these Maori women, photographed in New Zealand in 1903, are using the natural heat from geothermal springs to boil their kettles and cook food.
Photo: RGS

Under a roof of snow, and on the icy roof of the world. Left, an Inuit man puts the finishing touches to his igloo on Baffin Island, Canada. Above, Tenzing Norgay on the summit of Mount Everest in 1953. His ice-axe features the flags of Nepal, India, the United Nations and the UK. The picture was taken by Edmund Hillary.
Photos: Martha Holmes (left) and RGS (above)

Left: the mud towers of Shibam in Hadramout province, Yemen. The impressive structures look almost modern—it is hard to believe that these skyscrapers have stood for 300 years. Not for nothing is Shibam known as "the Manhattan of the desert".
Photo: Patrick Syder

Above, prehistoric cave paintings at Cueva de las Manos, "the cave of the hands", at Santa Cruz in Argentina. This place, like the skyscrapers of Shibam, has a strangely contemporary feel. You would not be surprised to see such stencil art as graffiti on an urban wall, or as a project in a classroom.
Photo: Eric Lawrie

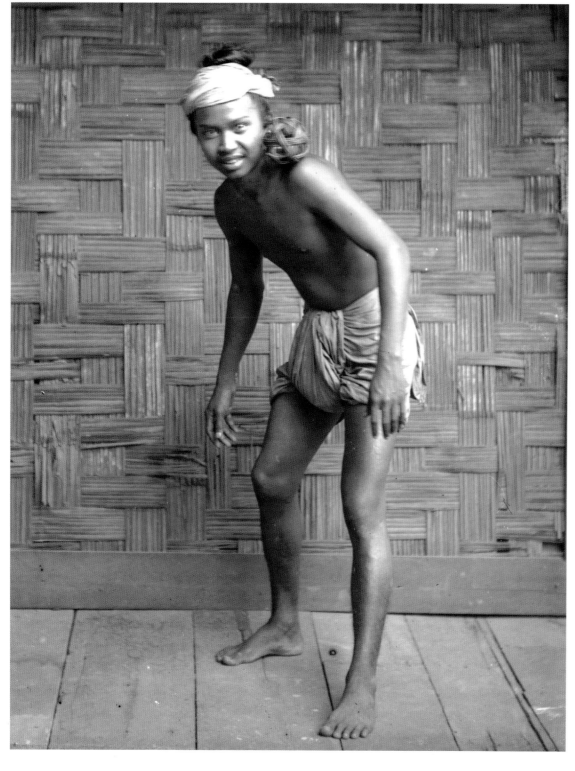

A young boxer poses for the camera of Max and Bertha Ferrars in Burma in the 1890s. Right, the colourful wares of the Indian garland seller are almost lost against the rich hue of the wall behind her.
Photos: RGS (above) and Stephen Coyne (right)

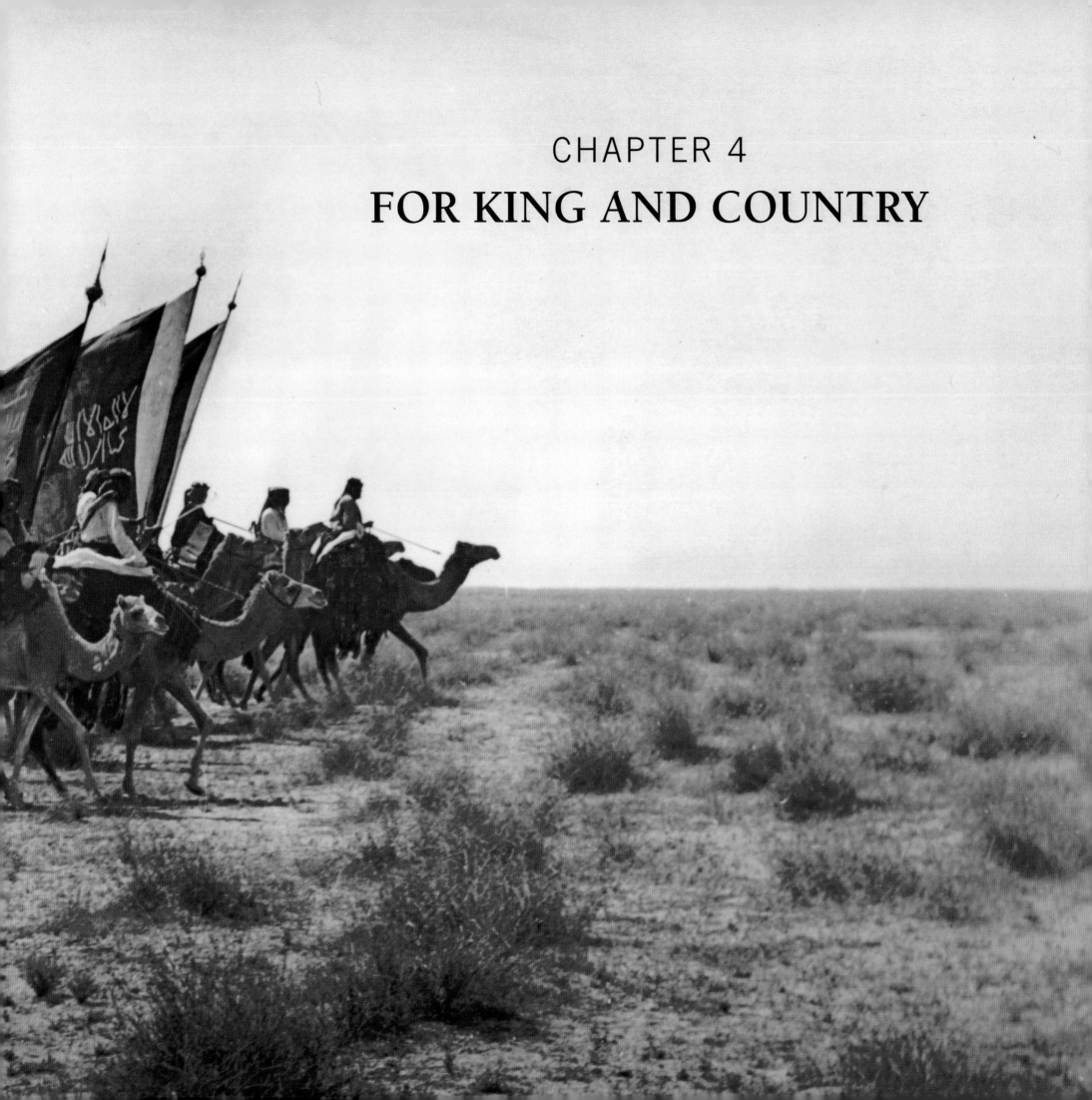

CHAPTER 4
FOR KING AND COUNTRY

FOR KING AND COUNTRY

Jonathan Bastable

The years before the First World War were a golden age of field geography. The British Empire was at its height, and everywhere on its fringes were uncharted and unexplored lands. One of these territories was the Arabian peninsula. This great rectangle of land—only slightly smaller in area than the Indian subcontinent—was an important focus of British diplomacy and of geographical exploration throughout the turbulent Edwardian decade, and then during the Great War.

The significance of Arabia lay in the fact that it formed a corridor between Europe and British India. The northern edge of the Arabian rectangle abuts the Mediterranean Sea, and so provides access to Europe. The longer southern edge lies on the Indian Ocean, its ports a sea-voyage away from India itself. Britain was in contact with the Arabs of the Gulf and Red Sea areas, but the endless inland deserts were a cartographic blank. To Europeans, they were almost as unknown and inhospitable as the surface of the moon. But as a matter of foreign policy, His Majesty's government needed to establish exactly who and what was there. Arabia also happened to contain many important archaeological sites waiting to be excavated or recorded. So the Empire required a set of "geographical spies", a handful of gifted and resourceful individuals who could penetrate these lands, make friends with their rulers and draw them gently into the British sphere of influence.

It so happened that Britain produced several such individuals all at once. Chief among them were Gertrude Bell, a freelance explorer with a passion for wilderness travel; Captain William Shakespear, an officer in the Bengal Lancers who spent long, lonely years as Britain's political officer in Kuwait; and Harry St John Bridger Philby, a maverick diplomat with an instinctive talent for discovery. These three devoted their lives to the Arabian Desert and its people, and each of them deposited a vivid and priceless legacy of documents and photographs in the archive of the Royal Geographical Society.

AL-KHATUN—"THE LADY"—RIDING BY

It was Gertrude Bell's immense good fortune to be born into a wealthy, well-connected family (Charles Dickens was a good friend of her father). All her life Bell used her private income and her highly placed contacts to further her aims as an archaeologist and geographer and as a friend of the Arabs of Mesopotamia.

But her life's achievements were all her own. She was a brilliant scholar who graduated with a First from Oxford in just five terms. She was an outstanding linguist and translator—her first public achievement was a fine translation of the medieval Persian poet Hafiz—and later in life she could converse freely in the many hoary and haughty dialects of Arabic. She became a wily diplomat once she placed her skills at the service of the British government; at the same time she was a wise counsellor to the Arabs whom she so admired. And all her life she was a meticulous archaeologist and a tireless traveller.

What is more, she never let herself be hindered by the fact that she was a woman in a man's world—not when she was with the frock-coated mandarins of the foreign service, and still less when she was drinking coffee in the tents of sheikhs. In fact, she turned her status as a woman into an unassailable advantage. It made her unique. "For a hundred years," said one Arab to her near the end of her life, "they will talk of *al-Khatun*— "The Lady"—riding by."

Previous page: Captain William Shakespear's image from 1911 of Ibn Saud's army on the march near Habl, Arabia.

Gertrude Bell was one of the most remarkable women of her age. She made outstanding contributions to many fields: poetry, diplomacy, archaeology, exploration and travel writing to name but a few.

Gertrude Bell was never happier than when enjoying the hospitality of the courteous nomadic Arabs. She took this photograph. It is a relaxed and thoughtful portrait of Fahad Bey, one of the most powerful sheikhs in the region.

Bell remained devoted to frontline archaeology throughout her life. This page from her notebooks is her survey of one of the ruined buildings at Binbirklisse, the city of a thousand and one churches.

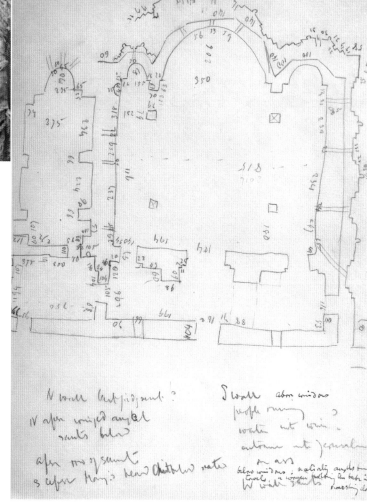

Bell first dipped a toe in the desert sands during an extended visit to Jerusalem in 1899. It was then that she began to learn Arabic. She took hundreds of photographs of the Holy City and the surrounding uplands. She also travelled to see the great ruins at Petra and Palmyra, and headed north to see Damascus and the cedars of Lebanon.

But these were mostly tourist trips—"Cook-ridden paths", she called them—and Bell's first steps as an independent explorer were taken not in the Judaean hills but in the Swiss Alps. Here, over the course of several summers, she tackled some previously unconquered peaks, one of which is named after her. Until she had a mountaineering suit made, she was wont to take off her heavy skirts and climb in her long underwear. Here, as later in the desert, practical common sense always won out over Victorian propriety.

Bell's desert travels began in earnest in 1905. "This is my first night in the desert," she exclaimed breathlessly, "the first of I wonder how many dozens, scores—Heaven knows!" She journeyed through Syria and on to Damascus once more, by now utterly infatuated with the mysterious sandscape of Arabia. Her published account of the experience reads

Right: Bell, photographed with colleagues at Baghdad station, fell in love with Mesopotamia as soon as she arrived there. "I like Baghdad and I like Iraq," she wrote. "It's the real East and it's stirring." She criss-crossed the land, looking for interesting ruins such as Kharaneh (far right), a maze-like Umayyad castle in the middle of the Jordanian steppe.

Gertrude Bell quickly learned the lore of the desert, and she knew how important it was to take good care of one's transport (opposite page). One wise Arab told her that, "if the water-skins break between water and water, or if the camel falls lame, the rider perishes."

in places like a love song to the desert: "The world of adventure and enterprise, dark with hurrying storms, glittering in raw sunlight, and unanswered question and unanswerable doubt hidden in the fold of every hill. The voice of the wind shall be heard instead of the persuasive voices of counsellors, the touch of the rain and the prick of the frost shall be spurs sharper than praise or blame."

From Damascus, Bell pushed on through Asia Minor to Binbirklisse, an early Christian city whose name means "a thousand and one churches". She made some drawings of the ruins and returned there two years later with the distinguished archaeologist Sir William Ramsay. Together they published a monograph on the ancient town. It was as well received as her earlier poetical translations. Bell's tattered, sandblown sketchbooks from Binbirklisse are in the archive of the RGS. Her pencil plans of the many ruins are drawn with an architect's precision; every wall has been measured out in paces and the distance noted on the sketches in tiny figures.

After the publication of *A Thousand and One Churches* Bell set off to explore Syria more fully. On this trip she made the architectural discovery of a lifetime: "An enormous castle, palace, fortress, what you will … the most undreamt of example of the finest Sassanian art that ever was. It is not seen on the map, it has never been published …" Bell had found it by listening closely to the talk of the Arabs who gathered at her fire, and by asking a lot of questions. These skills as an eavesdropper and a conversationalist were to stand her in good stead in her later career as a government agent.

But for now there were more desert places to be visited. She went to Babylon and to Baghdad—the city that would become her last home. She also visited a dig at the Abyssinian site of Carchemish. There she met a young English archaeologist who came to work each day in baggy football shorts and a dusty old blazer. His name was Tom Lawrence— "an interesting boy," noted Bell, "he will make a traveller." Her hunch was right, but it was as a military commander —Lawrence of Arabia—that the interesting boy found fame.

Bell made her last long desert trip in 1913. She was at the end of an unhappy love affair, and to soothe her own heart she trekked to the very heart of Arabia. "Already I have dropped back into the desert as if it were my own place," she wrote. "Silence and solitude fall around you like an impenetrable veil; there is no reality but the long hours of riding,

shivering in the morning and drowsy in the afternoon, the bustle of getting into camp, the talk round Muhammad's coffee fire after dinner, profounder sleep than civilisation ever knows—and then the road again. And as usual one feels secure and confident in this lawless country as one does in one's own village."

But this trip was not just a lover's escape. In the Arabian interior Bell gathered much information that was valuable to the British war effort in the Middle East. In 1915 she was officially co-opted into British military intelligence, for whom she wrote a series of reports on the political situation in Arabia. In 1917 she was installed as a political officer in Baghdad, and after the war she was summoned by Winston Churchill, then Colonial Secretary, to a conference at which the political future of Mesopotamia was decided. At that meeting in Cairo she was the only woman among 40 experts on the region.

When the new state of Iraq was created she was involved in the complex work of defining its borders—thereby adding her own political lines to the geographical contours that she had already contributed to the map. She also helped to identify Faisal, son of the Sharif of Mecca, as the preferred candidate for the throne of Iraq. Once he was crowned with Britain's blessing, she became his firm friend and close adviser. She was, by now, a real force in the newly minted Iraqi state, a kingmaker and a respected national figure: *al-Khatun*, "The Lady".

In the last years of her life, Bell returned to archaeology. She became King Faisal's "Director of Antiquities", and drafted a law on excavations in Iraq. She founded a museum in Baghdad where her adopted country's heritage could be exhibited. It is still there—and was, for a short time, the centre of the world's attention when it was reported that its riches had been looted in the chaotic aftermath of the fall of Saddam Hussein. This museum is part of Bell's enduring legacy—along with her writing, her scholarship and her travels. She was awarded the Royal Geographical Society's Gold Medal in 1918.

An inscribed rock photographed by Gertrude Bell during her travels in the Arabian Desert in 1916. One of her techniques for finding sites was to listen surreptitiously to the talk of local people who could not believe that she understood their language.

The ancient minaret at Samarra, Iraq (photographed by Frank Kingdon-Ward), has stood for more than a thousand years and is one of the country's finest monuments.

SHAKESPEAR OF ARABIA

While Bell was mapping her soul and gathering military intelligence in the Arabian north, a more prosaic spirit was doing the government's work in the south. Captain William Shakespear, Britain's political officer in Kuwait, was never troubled by the fact that he shared his name with England's greatest son. Rather than be cowed by the association, he set about carving out his own place in British history.

Shakespear accomplished this through his epic journeys into the Arabian interior. He was the first European to meet with the house of Saud, and he was to become a close friend of its ruler. Shakespear was no writer—in all his long journeys he never penned a vivid description nor described an emotion—but he was a first-class patriotic explorer in the tradition of men such as Sir Francis Drake and the Victorian adventurer Fred Burnaby. Like them, he lived for danger. He was also an almost obsessive photographer—there are boxes and boxes of his carefully labelled prints in the Royal Geographical Society archive, most of which he developed in the desert using the precious little water that was to hand.

Shakespear's first adventure was a pioneering solo jaunt. While he was on duty as a young consul in India he spent £250 on that new fangled thing, a motor car. He taught himself to drive on the mud tracks of Hyderabad, then had his car shipped to the British residency in southern Persia. Here he loaded up with a tent, a gun, cans of petrol and a large supply of tinned tongue, and set off for Teheran. From the Persian capital he proceeded into the roadless Zagros Mountains to Constantinople. He then coaxed his tired machine through Greece, Italy, Switzerland, France and thence to his parents' home in Brighton. It was a journey of well over 2000 miles (3200 km), and it made Shakespear's name.

Shakespear returned to India at the end of his leave, but in 1909, at the young age of 30, he was appointed to the post that would change his life. He became Britain's consul in the gulf port of Kuwait. His job was to observe the politics of the local Bedouin tribes (as shifting and unpredictable as the desert sands), and in particular to maintain friendly relations with Mubarak, Emir of Kuwait, who was an established ally of Britain.

To fulfill the first part of his brief, Shakespear made frequent short excursions into the desert, where he endeared himself to the sheikhs with his command of their language and customs, and with his skills as a hawker and huntsman. He was a regular and exotic visitor to their black tents.

As he grew acquainted with the desert, Shakespear became increasingly intrigued by the figure of Ibn Saud, the young emir of the unexplored central region of Arabia called the Najd. The emir was the political leader of the Wahabbis, a kind of puritan sect of Islam that advocated a return to the simple teachings of the Prophet. Shakespear seems to have seen Ibn Saud as the Oliver Cromwell of the desert—that is, as a man who could unite the Arabs through strength of personality, the might of arms, and the force of his uncompromising religious creed. He felt sure that the emir could become a useful ally of Britain against the decadent and failing Turkish Empire in the far north. He often shared this conviction with his superiors in London, who routinely dismissed it out of hand. Shakespear was eventually proved right, but did not live to see Ibn Saud become the first king of the country which still bears his family name: Saudi Arabia.

But a year after Shakespear's arrival in Arabia, the two men had still not even met. Their first encounter took place in 1910, when Ibn Saud came to see Mubarak in Kuwait. The Arab prince and the English consul, both in their early 30s, took an instant liking to each other. Ibn Saud permitted Shakespear to take his picture—the first known photographic portrait of the future king—and invited him to visit his capital at Riyadh, deep inside the Najd. Shakespear was delighted to accept. This was a diplomatic coup, and it fitted perfectly with a scheme that he had been harbouring for three years now: to be the first European to cross the vastness of Arabia from sea to sea, from his eastern base on the shores of the Arabian Gulf to the tip of the westerly Red Sea.

This is one of the first pictures of Ibn Saud, future ruler of Saudi Arabia. He is sitting on the left of the seated group of three. Next to him is Mubarak, Emir of Kuwait. The photograph was taken by William Shakespear at his residency in Kuwait in 1910.

Shakespear took many pictures of desert life. Here (opposite page) a nomadic Arab carries a baby camel in a saddle bag on its mother's back.

Four years were to pass before that epic journey came to fruition, but in the meantime each winter Shakespear probed deeper into the desert on exploratory forays. Every twist and turn of these journeys is recorded in his ruled notebooks, which are now part of the Royal Geographical Society archive. These books resemble accountants' ledgers, in which each day's miles are carried over like money in the bank. The books also have a column headed "Remarks," where the events of the day are recorded in sparse telegraphese: "30 Mar. Thursday. Left Camp XXXI, altered course, passed Arraifiya wells & altered course to Camp XXXII at Um-al-Hainan."

Shakespear assigned a consecutive Roman numeral to each night's camp, so it is clear that on this trip he had been in the desert for more than a month. Since so much of the Arabian interior was unmapped, government officers such as Shakespear were trained to take aneroid readings, to measure water's boiling point in order to calculate altitude, and to plot the size and position of wells and wadis using a sextant and the stars. Shakespear was as religious in this duty as his Arab guides were devoted to their prayers. For every day in the desert, his notes contain the vital set of readings—though sometimes his schoolboyish scrawl is barely legible. These pencil jottings were subsequently collated by the War Office and used to create the first serviceable maps of the Najd region.

On his expedition of 1911 Shakespear met up with Ibn Saud's nomadic entourage and cemented his friendship with the emir. They travelled together for several days, and on the way passed by the ruins of a place called Thaj. He spent some time copying strange angular letters that he found on tombstones, and photographed them too for good measure. His Arab companions were most amused to find their eccentric companion drawing rocks, but Shakespear—though no archaeologist—knew a find when he saw one. The inscriptions later confirmed that in the centuries before the Prophet there must have been a lively trade route running north from Yemen.

Shakespear finally made his great desert crossing in 1914. He set out from Kuwait with a retinue consisting of 10 guides and servants, 18 camels and 4 sheep. He was also equipped with a small armoury of rifles and letters of safe conduct signed by Ibn Saud—both intended to protect him from the suspicious and marauding Bedouins that he was bound to meet along the way.

He first headed southwest to the arc of corrugated sand mountains called the Dahana. At this natural barrier, he turned sharp left towards Riyadh. This was a detour of several hundred miles, but Shakespear wanted to visit his royal friend in his palace. He spent many days as the guest of the emir, during which time he rode out with him under the Saudi war flag, and

Shakespear was shocked to find himself a witness to a desert execution. The condemned man, barely more than a boy, is holding the dish into which his blood will be spilt. He looks up and smiles at the foreigner with the strange lens. Seconds later he is dead.

Far right: one of the first known photographs of Riyadh was taken by Captain Shakespear in 1914. The panorama shows a view of the great street looking west from the east gate. The city wall can be seen on the right-hand side of the image.

took the first photographs of Riyadh. These pictures are a striking record of the city before oil money transformed it from a clay citadel into a modern metropolis. In these days, according to the historian H. V. F. Winstone, the emir "was said to be able to carry the entire wealth of central Arabia in gold pieces in saddle bags."

A few westerners had seen Riyadh before Shakespear (though none had been made so welcome). But soon after striking out northwest once more, Shakespear was in unexplored territory. As ever, he took his readings each day at noon, writing his diary and developing his photographic plates in the dark of the desert night. During the days he pressed on, battling sandstorms, stomach cramps, fractious and indolent guides, toothache (he extracted one of his own molars with a pair of rusty pliers), swarms of locusts and bands of thieves. As his caravan got beyond the lands where Ibn Saud was feared, the party took to travelling at night, and refrained from erecting their tents to avoid being seen by hostile tribesmen.

Once they came upon the old north-south pilgrim route from Damascus to Mecca, Shakespear knew he was nearing his goal. The last stage of the journey led along the northern edge of Sinai's inverted triangle, at the far end of which was British-controlled Cairo. The Great Pyramid at Giza marked the end of Shakespear's desert odyssey.

Exhausted, Shakespear sailed home to Britain for a period of furlough. He lodged his notes and pictures with the Royal Geographical Society, was elected a Fellow and gave a lecture. He was expecting to be posted back to India, but that autumn the great machinery of world conflict creaked into motion. Now, at last, Britain gave a measure of support to Ibn Saud as a natural enemy of the pro-German Turks. Shakespear was instantly packed off to Arabia to tell him.

Shakespear caught up with Ibn Saud in the desert on New Year's Eve, 1914. The emir was then at the head of his army, marching to do battle with his old enemy and northern ally of the Turks, Ibn Rashid. Shakespear stayed close to Ibn Saud, using the time at his side to explain his government's changing policy.

The two Arab armies clashed at a place called Jarab. Ibn Saud did not want Shakespear to witness the battle. But Shakespear insisted on being present so that he could report back to London on its outcome. He was also loath to miss the excitement. Shakespear was shot dead while aiming his camera at Ibn Saud's camel cavalry and simultaneously firing his revolver at Ibn Rashid's advancing forces.

A letter was subsequently sent by the new political officer in Kuwait to Shakespear's younger brother. "Dear Shakespear," it read. "I am very sorry to tell you that your brother was killed in a tribal fight in the interior about 180 miles from here on 14th January. We have only just received the news … The government has every reason to be grateful for the work your brother did here. It was recognised by the CIE [Companion of the Order of the Indian Empire], the news of the grant of which I am afraid never reached him."

Captain Shakespear's name is less renowned than it deserves to be. Had history taken a slightly different turn he, rather than T. E. Lawrence, might have become the great British champion of Arab independence.

Overleaf: this picture of Mecca during the pilgrimage was taken from inside the King's Palace by Harry St John Philby. He was not allowed to visit the city until he converted to Islam.

GREATEST OF ARABIAN EXPLORERS

Shakespear had always refused to wear Arab costume. He was an officer in the Indian army, and as a point of principle he wore his captain's uniform throughout his years in Arabia. (This sartorial quirk may have made him too tempting a target at the battle of Jarab.) Harry St John Philby, the man who succeeded Shakespear as Ibn Saud's English confidant, was a very different character—almost a mirror image in personality and approach. Philby not only delighted in dressing like an Arab, but also did his level best to become an Arab, or at least to be indistinguishable from an Arab in every way. Later in life he became a Muslim—though this was prompted as much by his explorer's ambition to go to places such as Mecca, which were closed to unbelievers, as it was by a convert's change of heart.

The death of Shakespear had left Britain without a voice at the court of Ibn Saud. The British government decided to send Philby, who was then working in Mesopotamia alongside Gertrude Bell. Like her, he served under Percy Cox, chief political officer and later British high commissioner in Baghdad. Philby's mission was the same as Shakespear's: to represent the British view to Ibn Saud. He was to ask the emir to send an army against the pro-Turkish Arabs to the north, and also to cease his longstanding quarrel with the Sharif of Mecca. The sharif ruled the western part of Arabia known as the Hijaz, and had, with British support, declared himself "King of the Arabs"—much to Ibn Saud's annoyance.

Aircraft, such as that shown opposite, were useful tools in the mapping of the Middle East enabling many previously uncharted areas to be surveyed.

Philby, like Gertrude Bell, delighted in the company of Arab people. This picture (below) is a family snapshot of Sultan ibn Manif of the clan of Yam.

Mecca, the birthplace of the Prophet Muhammad, was conquered by the house of Saud after the collapse of the Ottoman Empire. Oil was first shipped from this part of western Arabia a year or two after Harry Philby took this picture of the rooftops of the holy city. The Kaaba can be seen on the left.

Once in Riyadh, Philby quickly hit it off with Ibn Saud, just as Shakespear had done before him. Philby did not hesitate to make the most of his new acquaintance for his own ends. He convinced himself and the emir that it would help matters if he were to make the trip west to the Hijaz to meet the sharif. This proposal was highly dubious from a diplomatic point of view, but it would give Philby the chance to traverse the uncharted southern reaches of the Najd. The prospect of this adventure blotted out all considerations of duty.

Philby sent a message to Cox in Baghdad asking for permission to undertake the journey. He then set off before there was any chance of a refusal reaching him—a favourite ruse throughout his years of government service. This trip was his first opportunity to immerse himself in the life of the desert Arabs. He grew a beard, ate mutton and rice with his guides, listened to their tales around the fire at night and grew very attached to his riding camel. When the party met unfriendly Bedouin tribes he kept in the background so as not to give himself away as a European and an infidel—but none of the Arabs he encountered ever suspected that he was not a born son of the desert.

Philby reached the Red Sea in triumph, was received by the sharif, and then officially rebuked by Cox. He also received a sharp telling-off in a letter from Gertrude Bell, who always treated the younger explorer as a naughty boy in need of a nanny. Upbraided but rather proud of himself, Philby was shipped to Cairo and then back to Baghdad.

But Philby's knowledge and burgeoning acquaintance with Ibn Saud were too valuable to waste. He was soon sent back to Riyadh to build his friendship with the emir and use it to Britain's advantage. But he arrived at Ibn Saud's court during Ramadan. There was no hope of engaging the emir in serious political business at this time—a circumstance that Philby saw as another heaven-sent opportunity. Rather than sit in Riyadh doing nothing, he asked Ibn Saud for an escort to take him south into areas of the Najd that no European had seen before. Firing off another of his too-late-to-stop-me telegrams, and equipped with new surveying instruments bought in Cairo, he absented himself from his post for the best part of two months. During this period he penetrated as far as the town of Dam, at the point where the dry river bed of Wadi Dawasir bisects the mountain range of Jabal Tuwaiq. This passage through the rocky highlands was once the trade route into central Arabia for coffee caravans from the southern coast.

The High Commission was furious with Philby for going off exploring when he should have been working, but the Royal Geographical Society was delighted. The information he gathered was so fine and voluminous that they awarded him the founder's medal. His work allowed the first accurate maps of this part of Arabia to be compiled. If Philby had never ventured into the desert again, his legacy as a geographer would have been assured. But his most spectacular journey was still more than a decade ahead of him.

The 1920s were hard years for Philby. He was still indispensable, but he became increasingly disillusioned with the British government's policy towards Arabia. To the fury of his superiors, he wrote many newspaper articles saying so while still on the government payroll. During these years he nursed a dream that became an obsession. He wanted to be the first European to cross the immense wilderness in the far south of Arabia known as Rub al-Khali, the "Empty Quarter".

So Philby left the civil service for good. He moved to Jidda, where he became a courtier and unofficial adviser to Ibn Saud, by now King of Saudi Arabia. In the summer of 1930 the king summoned him to Mecca. In the holy city, the former diplomat ceremoniously kissed the *Kaaba*—the black stone given to Abraham by the angel Gabriel—and thus became a Muslim. He took the name Hajj Abdullah.

Philby's new faith allowed him to enter fully into the Arab way of life, but it in no way dimmed his old European yearning for exploration. He now used his position at the king's side to lobby for permission to go into the Empty Quarter. The king refused this favour for months, but in the end Philby's persistence wore him down. He told the explorer that he could go, and promised to provide men and beasts for the trip.

In January 1932, Philby set out from Hufuf near Qatar with 32 camels and enough provisions to last for three months. This was perhaps his most arduous journey. He trained for it by going for days without water. But the Empty Quarter, despite its name, yielded many finds and precious experiences. Among them were the "singing sands". In one large, curved dune near Naifa, Philby and his guides heard a mysterious deep thrumming noise "like an aeroplane engine". Philby supposed that a small landslide had caused the sandbowl to resonate like a struck bell; his superstitious Arab companions put the sound down to the evil spirits known as *djinns*.

Philby remained in the service of the king for the next three decades, during which time he was often commissioned by the Saudi government to undertake desert expeditions. He surveyed the kingdom's southern border, and also ventured north, where he rooted out pre-Islamic ruins and inscriptions. Like a boy with an unfinished jigsaw puzzle, he used these journeys to fill in some of the large blanks on his own maps of the desert. This was a work still in progress when he died in 1960. The epitaph for Philby's gravestone was written by his son Kim. The words might equally have been claimed by Gertrude Bell or Captain Shakespear. It reads: "Greatest of Arabian explorers".

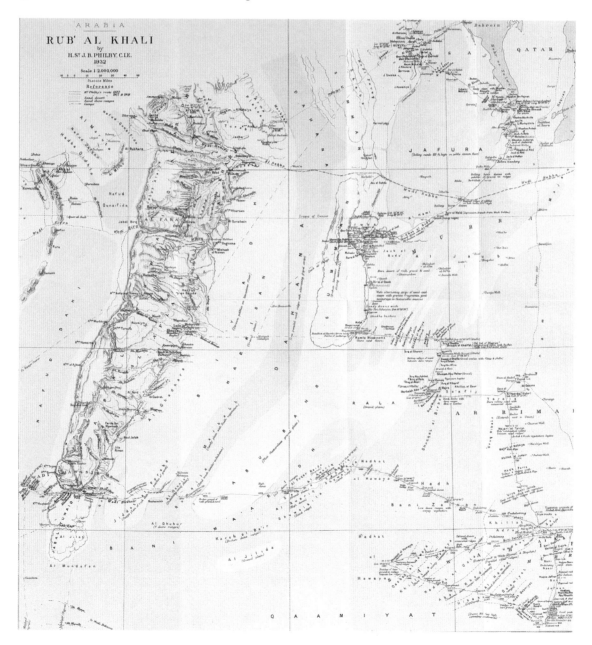

Philby provided the information for this map of Rub al-Khali (right), the Empty Quarter, in 1932. Like Livingstone in Africa, he sketched in the geography of a region that was almost entirely unmapped before that time.

Philby was fascinated by the life of the desert: by its people, by the sculptural shapes that the wind made of the sand and by its fauna. He was, among other things, a talented ornithologist, and several new species of bird were given their names by Philby.

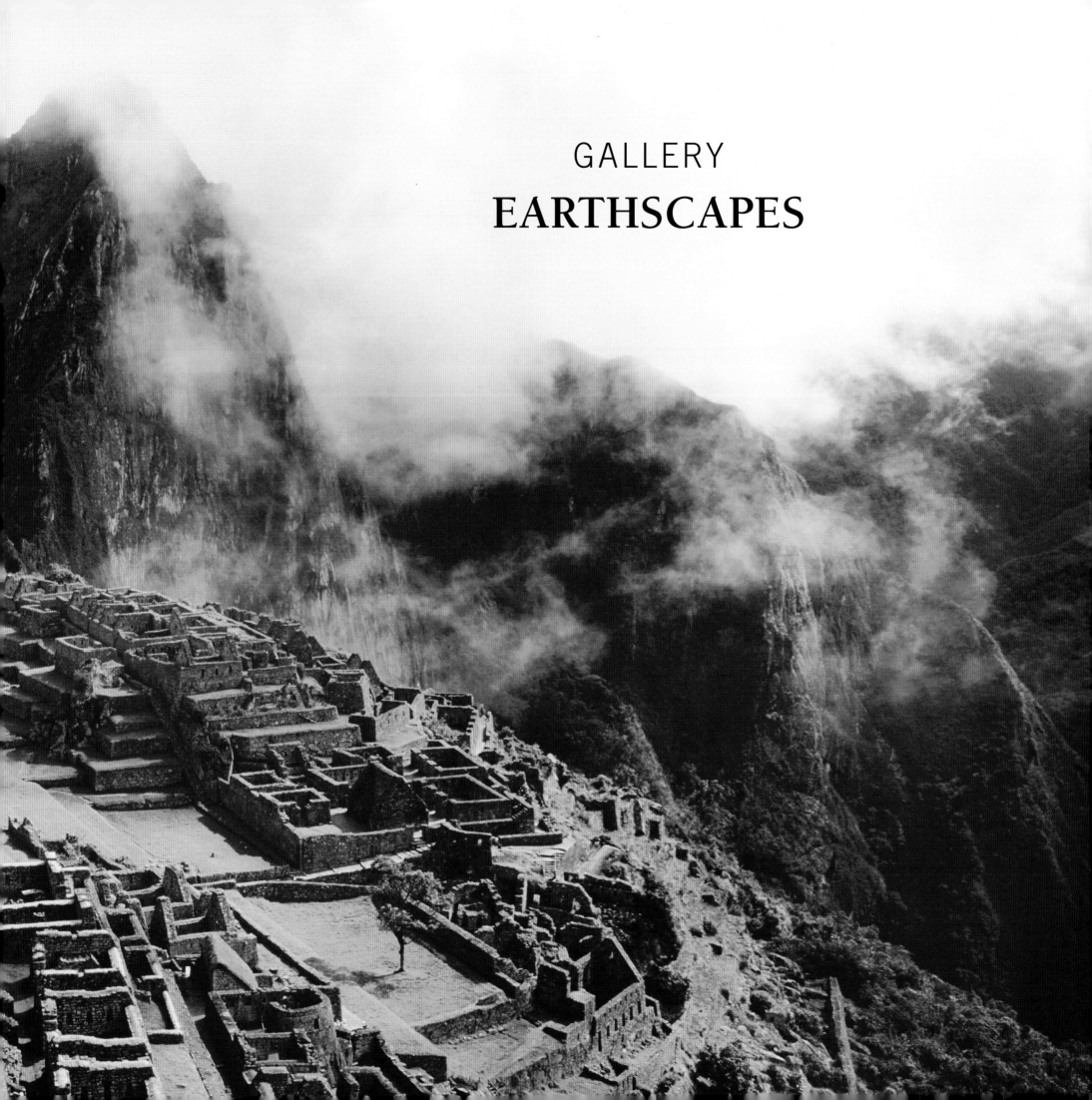

GALLERY
EARTHSCAPES

Pages 140–141: The Inca ruins of Machu Picchu were discovered by Hiram Bingham in 1911. Then the complex of buildings was almost submerged in the dense Peruvian rainforest. It is a long climb to the point where the jungle parts like a green curtain to reveal the fantastic ziggurats of the city.
Photo: Chris Caldicott

The sand dunes of the Kalahari, in eastern Namibia, opposite page. The crest of the dune looks like the edge of a giant flint; it has been sharpened to a point by the whetting action of the wind.
Photo: Brenda Friel

The snowy summit of Monte Sarmiento, left, is the highest point in Tierra del Fuego, the archipelago that forms the curly tail of South America. The mountain stands 7,887 feet (2,404 m) high. From its peak there are views across the Cockburn Channel to the ragged islands of the Patagonian coast.
Photo: Stephen Venables

The shadowy forms of the
Yangshuo mountains, left, in
southwest China appear flat and
unreal, like painted scenery within
the proscenium arch of a cave.
Photo: Chris Caldicott

An image of Buddhist stupas,
above, taken in the 1890s in
Burma. The first stupas were little
more than mounds of clay or mud,
intended to cover relics of the
Buddha. Over time the construction
of a stupa became a religious act,
and they grew in size and
complexity. Some, like these, are
refined architectural edifices.
Photos: Max and Bertha Ferrars/RGS

Petra, an astonishing collection
of temples hewn from the rock, was
memorably described as "the rose
red city, half as old as time". John
Burgon, who wrote those words,
never went to Petra. In fact, few
of the buildings are pink, and they
are a mere 2,500 years old. The
so-called "monastery" (right) is
set deep in the cliff—an indication
of how much rock was chipped
away to create its pillared façade.
The dramatic eastern approach
(opposite) to the Khazneh
or "treasury" is through a narrow
gorge called the Siq (Arabic
for "shaft").

Photos: Alexander Kennedy/RGS (right)
and Chris Caldicott (opposite)

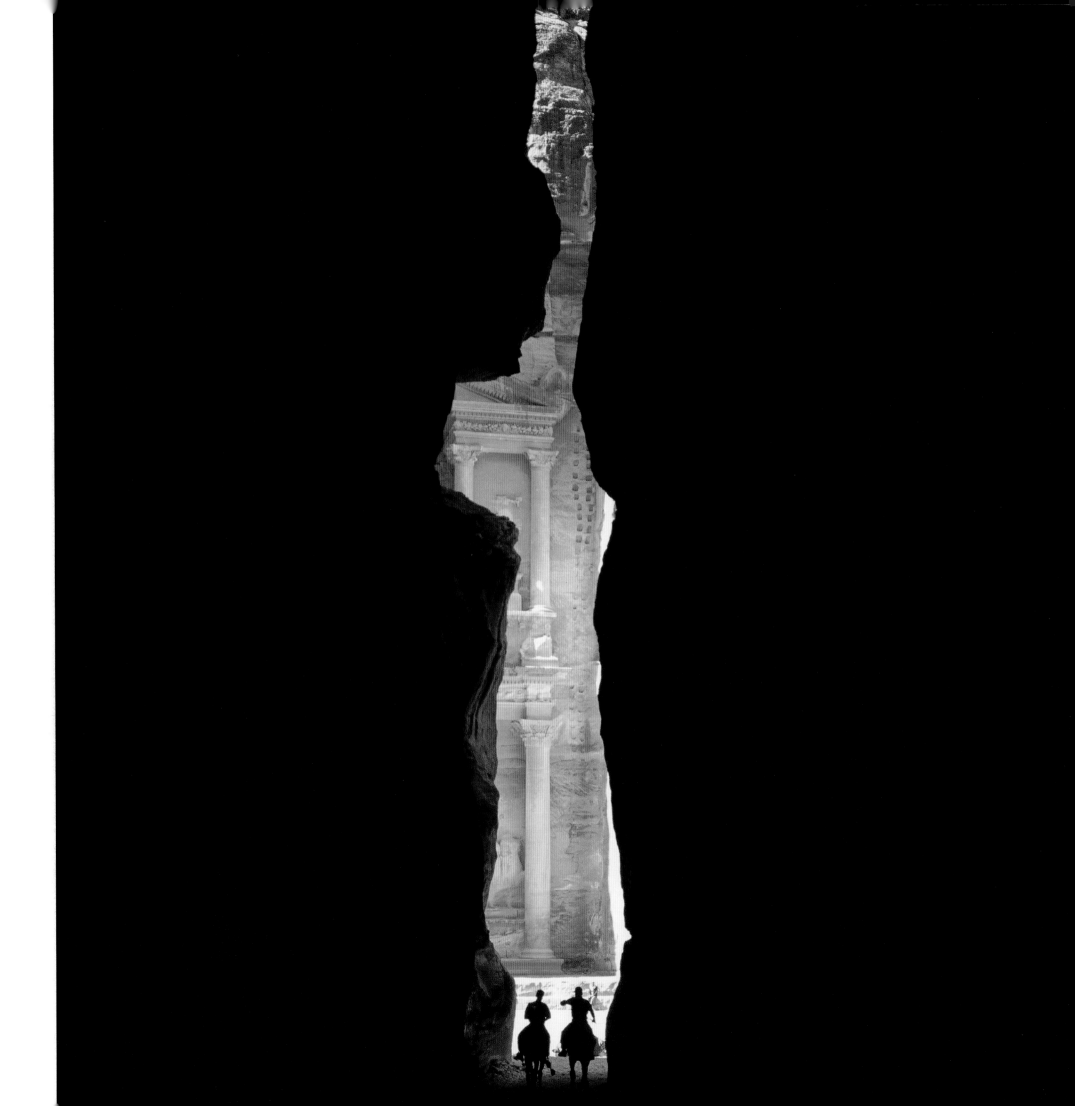

Termite mounds come in a surprising variety of shapes and sizes. These mounds, above, in the Australian desert near Kimberley, have the look of an architectural ensemble: they are a collection of miniature skyscrapers, each one filled with diligent insect workers.
Photo: Joann Crowther

This thermal lake, right, in New Zealand looks as warm and inviting as a hot bath. The orange fringe is caused by rock-borne minerals which dissolve in the water. They are then deposited, like limescale in a kettle, as the shallowest water at the edge of the pool evaporates.
Photo: Chris Wright

This Vietnamese junk (below) is instantly recognizable by its butterfly-wing sails. It is hugging the coast just off Ha Long Bay. Eight thousand miles away, in the warm waters off Kenya, a two-man dhow (right) keeps land in sight in much the same way.

Photos: John R. Jones (below) and Robert Maletta (right)

At Gauthgame Point on the west coast of Australia, the wind licks the sandstone outcrops into strange sculptural shapes, while the sea gnaws at the base of the cliff. In some places, where the layers of stone have been stripped away, fossilized dinosaur footprints are revealed.
Photo: Joann Crowther

Exploration has changed since this plateau iceberg caught the eye of Herbert Ponting at Cape Royd, Antarctica. Now every continent has been opened, and the challenge is to explore in new ways. In 1979 Fiennes's Transglobe Expedition was the first to pass through both poles. In the south, Fiennes walked in the footsteps of Scott; at the other end of the world, deep inside the Arctic, the footsteps were made by Fiennes's dog, Bothy.
Photos: Herbert Ponting/RGS (left) and Sir Ranulph Fiennes (above)

Overleaf, retreating glaciers strew rocks and boulders in their wake. This great stone in the Biafo Glacier table, India, seems to have been deliberately placed on a rock point like a golf ball on a tee.
Photo: Steve Razzetti

No two sunsets are ever alike.
The coolly reflective lakeside scene,
(left) was taken at Findhorn Bay
near Forres in Scotland; the hot
orange sky looks down on
Zimbabwe (above).
Photos: Bruce Herrod (left) and Chris
Caldicott (above)

The sandstone Elephant Rock at Al-Ula is a popular tourist attraction in Saudi Arabia. Its strangely comical form has been created by sandstorms over thousands of years.
Photo: Stephen Coyne

This type of iceberg is called a sharkfin—and, as with real sharks' fins, what lies beneath the surface can be deadly. The floating Antarctic ice mountains are as solid as rock, easily hard enough to tear a fatal gash in the hull of a ship.
Photos: Martha Holmes

Overleaf: dating from the 10th century, the ancient ruins of Polonnaruwa are sited just north of the present-day town of the same name in Sri Lanka. The reclining Buddha is 46 feet (14 m) long while the standing statue alongside is 23 feet (7 m) tall.
Photo: David Constantine

The American photographer Carleton Watkins (1829–1916) made several stereographic prints of the Yosemite Valley, California, in the 1860s. Among the images in the RGS archive are Mirror Lake, right, and the majestic triple peak known as the Three Brothers, far right, which is 4480 feet (1336 m) tall at its highest point.
Photo: Carleton Watkins/RGS.

The fluted azure dome of Tamerlane's tomb, in the Uzbek city of Samarqand, is one of the jewels of Muslim architecture. Tamerlane, known as Timur in Central Asia, was a Mongol warlord who conquered Persia and northern India, and died leading his armies against China.
Photo: Sybil Sassoon/RGS

A collection of Hindu divinities populate the façade of this temple in Penang, Malaysia, in a similar way to the Christian saints and martyrs that crowd the outer walls of Gothic cathedrals.
Photo: Chris Caldicott

This bowl-shaped valley lies more than two miles above sea level, high in the mountain of India's Himachal Pradesh province. A tiny figure can be seen taking a drink at the water's edge.
Photo: Nick Eakins

Hippopotami jostle for position in the waters of the Luangwa River, Zambia. Meanwhile in Kenya, three baby elephants form an orderly queue in which the oldest goes first.
Photos: Martha Holmes (above) and Chris Caldicott (right)

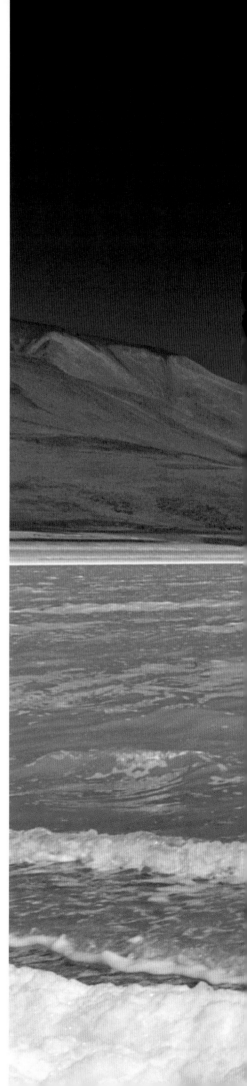

A polar bear swims toward an ice-floe in Wager Bay, on the northwest coast of Canada's Hudson Bay. Polar bears are believed to be threatened, not by hunting, but by the loss of habitat caused by global warming; for example, the area of ice covering the Hudson Bay in winter is shrinking, limiting access to prey such as seal.
Photo: Martha Holmes

The salt lake, right, at Laguna Verde, Bolivia. The Licancabur volcano, also pictured, contains a crater lake at its summit which at 19,422 feet (5920 m) is the highest lake in the world.
Photo: Eric Lawrie

A moonlit night in Rio de Janeiro in the 1920s, far left. Sugar Loaf Mountain can be seen looming over one of the largest natural harbours in the world. At the time this image was taken the population of the city had already reached 1,400,000 people.
Photo: RGS/Bippus Rio

The Iguazú Falls, left, lie on the border between Argentina and Brazil. They are actually a series of falls, stacked on top of each other to form a kind of watery staircase. One of the most impressive of them is known as La Garganta del Diablo—"The Devil's Throat".
Photo: Lina Fuller

The temple of Angkor Wat, Cambodia, left and detail above, was built for King Suryavarman II in the 12th century AD. It was his state temple and capital city. As the largest and best-preserved temple at Angkor, it has remained a religious centre since its foundation, used first by Hindus and then by Buddhists. It is the tradition among pilgrims to leave images of the Buddha in Preah Poan—the "Hall of a Thousand Buddhas".

Photos: Patrick Syder (left) and Sybil Sassoon (above)

Mount Fuji, above, as seen from Owakudani. At 12,388 feet (3,776 m), it is the highest of Japan's mountains. It is also an active volcano; the last recorded eruption was in 1707.
Photo: Bruce Herrod

The Great Wall of China, right, pictured in 1907. Most of the wall was built in the 15th century during the Ming Dynasty. Its function was to protect China from raids by Mongol and Turkic tribes.
Photo: Herbert Ponting/RGS

Overleaf: Hong Kong Island and Kowloon as seen from Victoria Peak at 1,811 feet (552 m), and, following page, Mount Everest as photographed on an expedition in 1935.
Photos: Stuart Crump (pages 180–181) and L. V. Bryant/RGS (pages 182–183)

CHAPTER 5

COLLECTING FOR THE FUTURE

COLLECTING FOR THE FUTURE

Jonathan Bastable

Previous page: mists over the Belalong forest during the Brunei Rainforest Project in which the RGS was involved between 1991–92.
Photo: Paul Harris

Frank Kingdon-Ward (below) was a small man, but he was also extremely tough. More than once on his travels he had to impose his authority on mutinous bearers by fighting them to a standstill.

The gorge of the Tsangpo River (opposite) constitutes some of the most difficult terrain in the world. Kingdon-Ward penetrated further than any man before him.

Most explorers are born hoarders. Part of the point of exploration and field science has always been to collect interesting things and bring them home. Moon rocks, beetles, artefacts, vocabularies, soil samples, folk art—it doesn't matter. All of these things are gathered by intrepid people with the same numismatic mentality. And back in Britain, explorers' sealed boxes, whatever they contain, become databanks—raw scientific material to be studied down the years by less footloose types in museums and in learned institutions such as the Royal Geographical Society.

Perhaps the most obsessive and romantic of all explorer-gatherers were the plant-hunters. These were men who spent their lives—and very often risked their lives—in the apparently effete pastime of picking wild flowers. They were horticultural buccaneers whose job it was to seek out treasures in dangerous and hostile lands, to find floral booty with which to fill the coffers of their sponsors—for newly discovered garden plants were big business as well as frontline botany. The profession practically became extinct after the Second World War, when the changed geopolitical scene made it impossible for British subjects to wander freely in the wilds of Asia. But before that, the best and last of the plant-hunters was Frank Kingdon-Ward.

INTO THE LAND OF FLOWERS

Francis Kingdon-Ward was born of good Victorian stock in Manchester in 1885. Kingdon was originally his middle name, taken from his mother's maiden name—she was distantly related to the great engineer Isambard Kingdom Brunel—but he later incorporated it into his surname. Francis's father, Harry Marshall Ward, was a professor of botany, so plant-spotting came to him as early and as naturally as speech. When he was still very young he overheard a visitor from India say to his father: "There are places up the Brahmaputra where no white man has ever been." Something about that remark, though he could barely have understood it, was ineffably exciting to the small boy. It awoke the latent explorer in him, or perhaps it planted an adventurous seed in his soul. At any rate, the words stayed with him, and in due course Kingdon-Ward would tackle some of the unseen stretches of that mysterious Asian river.

Though his interests and ambitions were in place early on, Kingdon-Ward's career got off to a slow start. When he was in his second year at Cambridge University his father died, and Frank had to leave his studies and earn money to support his mother and sister. He took a job as a teacher in Shanghai. Despite the exotic location, it was for him pure drudgery. To escape the boredom he took time off to join an American zoological expedition to Tibet.

This was his apprenticeship as an explorer; it was also his first visit to the land that would enchant him all his life. Years later he wrote a paean to Tibet, which reads like a kind of explorers' manifesto: "I believe I should be content to wander over it for years," he said. "To climb its rugged peaks, and tramp its deep snows, to fight its storms of wind and rain, to roam in the warmth of its deep gorges within sight and sound of its roaring rivers, and above all to mingle with its hardy tribesmen, is to feel the blood coursing through the veins, every nerve steady, every muscle taut."

Kingdon-Ward returned to the classroom, but not for long. In 1911 he was offered a job as a China-based collector of plants for the American seed company, Bees. He realized that he could practise botany as a money-making job, while at the same time indulging his passion for solitary exploration. The pattern of his life was now set.

Inexperienced as he was, Kingdon-Ward's first solo expedition was a great success. He brought back more than 200 species, about 20 of which were new discoveries. As well as fulfilling his contract with Bees, he made a useful contribution to the herbarium at Kew Gardens. The scientific work was exacting and laborious. For Kew, Kingdon-Ward had to provide a flowering specimen and the same plant in fruit; the specimens had to be sorted, pressed, dried, mounted on paper; and they had to be regularly unpacked and dusted with a soft paintbrush to protect them from mildew. Seeds also had to be dried, labelled, and stowed away in sponge bags or biscuit tins. Bulbs had to be embedded in soil and packed in woven baskets. And, of course, all of this had to be done in field conditions: at night, by the light of a camp fire, whatever the weather, no matter how ill or exhausted the plant-hunter.

Back in England, Kingdon-Ward was elected Fellow of the Royal Geographical Society at the young age of 26. The Society undertook to help him with his next expedition by providing him with surveying equipment and giving him lessons in the use of it. Unusually for an explorer, Kingdon-Ward was not much interested in map-making, and never really got the hang of his shiny new instruments. In his letters to the RGS, Kingdon-Ward regularly apologizes for botching his readings or for failing to take them altogether. The Society seems not to have held this against him, and on later trips Kingdon-Ward, for his part, often took a younger companion with him to do the geographical donkeywork. This allowed him to concentrate on scanning the earth beneath his feet or the mountainside up ahead for new botanical jewels.

An expedition in 1924 took him to the Tsangpo River in the land Tibetans call "the Land of Flowers". The Tsangpo constitutes the higher reaches of the Brahmaputra, the name of which so fired Kingdon-Ward's ambitions. It cuts like a cheesewire through the Himalayas, creating the deepest gorge in the world. The cliffs to either side are so high and narrow that they are all but impassable, and the course of the river is eternally sunless. Tibetan legend says that lost within the gorge are 75 waterfalls guarded by 75 spirits. The last of the falls is the largest, and beyond its veil lies a sunlit paradise.

Certainly the height of the river falls dramatically between the gorge and the point where it emerges as the Brahmaputra on the Assam Plain, so there ought to have been some spectacular waterfalls. Kingdon-Ward set out to test the legend, and to gather flowers along the way. He penetrated further into the gorge than anyone before him, but could not connect with the explored lower reaches before he had to turn back. He found some falls, wreathed in rainbows, but none so dramatic as the legend suggested. Since there now remained only a 5-mile (8-km) stretch of river that had not been seen by European eyes, Kingdon-Ward wrote off the great waterfall as a "romance of geography". It was left to

Frank Kingdon-Ward's albums, held in the RGS's archive, contain many images of plants photographed during his travels in the Far East (right and below). The striking Amorphophallus, shown far right, is from the Shan States, Burma.

This majestic bird is a trained vulture, tethered to a stake for safety's sake in Yunnan province, China.

Some of Kingdon-Ward's best pictures are of people. He had an eye for an interesting face, just as he could spot an intriguing botanical specimen. In his caption to the picture of the Tibetan girl (opposite page) he says that she was somewhat startled by the camera. Sadly, he did not record the great joke he shared with this Naga woman in Burma (left).

The lives of these children were already mapped out when Frank Kingdon-Ward took their pictures. The young Tibetan boy is a monk, equipped with his prayer wheel and beads. The Kaw girls in Laos are traders, carrying their wares to market on their backs.

Opposite, a man carries his dog across an elaborate cane bridge.

others to make something of that romance: James Hilton's novel *Lost Horizon*, with its tale of the fabled land of Shangri-La, was inspired by the Tibetan story and by Kingdon-Ward's journey.

For Kingdon-Ward the tangible result of the expedition was a sensational flower: the Tibetan Blue Poppy (*Meconopsis betonicifolia*). Its mere existence brought an award from the Royal Horticultural Society in 1926; it drew crowds when it was planted in large swathes in Hyde Park; and at the Chelsea Flower Show in 1927 seedlings sold for a guinea a piece. It made Kingdon-Ward's name as a botanist, and recognition as an explorer came soon after. He received the Royal Geographical Society's Gold Medal in 1930.

The Blue Poppy was one of many triumphs. But the one that delighted him most was perhaps the plant he called the Tea Rose Primula. His description of his first glimpse of it has the same ecstatic tone as Howard Carter's account of opening the tomb of Tutankhamun. "I had scarcely reached the bank when I stopped suddenly in amazement," wrote Kingdon-Ward. "Was I dreaming? I rubbed my eyes and looked again. No! Just above the edge of the snow a vivid, blush-pink flower stood out of the cold grey earth. It was as big as a rose, and of that fresh clear pink seen in *Madame Butterfly*. Of course it could not really be a rose, but what could it be? I just stood transfixed on the snow cone, in a honeymoon of bliss, feasting my eyes on a masterpiece. The vulgar thought—is it new?—did not at this moment occur to me. It was enough for me that I had never set eyes on it. Overcome by emotion, I could state no fact about the plant, apart from its sheer colour and brilliance."

Like Adam in the Garden of Eden, Kingdon-Ward took the greatest of pleasure in giving names to what were for him newly minted creations. Among his vivid coinages—all of them rhododendrons—were the "Coals of Fire", "Orange Bill", "Yellow Peril", and "Plum Warner", which, when he first encountered it, had "absurd little plummy mouths pouting discontentedly at us".

This kind of description is not twee anthropomorphism. Kingdon-Ward was keenly aware of the real personality of the places he travelled to and the things he found in them. He knew that there was a vital and palpable relationship between a landscape, its flora, fauna and human inhabitants. The study of these relationships is the modern discipline of ecology, and it has been said that Kingdon-Ward had all the instincts and interests of an ecologist before the term had even been invented. And so he was not just the last of a dying breed; he was also a man ahead of his time.

The small boy (below) in the eastern Himalayas, caught Kingdon-Ward's eye because he was carrying his baby brother. Other children (below right) pose for his camera on the supports of a house.

HENRY HAMILTON JOHNSTON

One of Kingdon-Ward's most interesting deposits in the archive of the Royal Geographical Society is a large collection of ethnographic photographs. Everywhere he went, he or one of his colleagues took pictures of the local people, and some of these are beautiful human studies that could pass for high art. But Kingdon-Ward was not the first to take an interest in this kind of ethnographic portraiture. Thomas Baines—Livingstone's erstwhile companion—made drawings of many of the characters he met on his travels; and so did another remarkable artist and Africanist: Henry Hamilton Johnston.

Harry Johnston's artistic gift manifested itself at the age of 10. He first picked up a pencil to while away the months spent at home as he recovered from scarlet fever. Birds and animals were his preferred subject from the very start, and throughout his teens he spent every spare afternoon at London Zoo, drawing its inhabitants. His talent brought him to the attention of the zoo's director, who gave him an introduction to the Royal College of Surgeons. Here he learned to draw human anatomy. In 1876, at the age 18, he entered the Royal Academy to study painting.

The impression of precocity that Johnston made on his elders was due in part to his extremely youthful appearance. Even as a grown man he stood just 5 feet 3 inches (1.6 m) tall; he had a high-pitched, childlike voice; and his face, even when adorned with a bushy Victorian moustache, was always a picture of puppyish wonder. When something interested him, he went at it with a boyish enthusiasm, and all his life he was prone to facetious behaviour that in a young person would be called naughtiness.

This self-portrait was taken by Harry Johnston in Ruwenzori, Uganda, in 1900.

But he was also charming, and he used this trait to get what he wanted. While still a student he persuaded his father to finance a long working trip abroad. He went to spend a joyous winter in Tunis—his first step into Africa—and he passed his days on an island in the lagoon, painting its herons and flamingoes as they were "slowly returning to the island to plume themselves, to forage, to quarrel or make love". He filled many notebooks with sketches of the souk outside his front door, and of the purple dragon's tail of the distant mountains. Taken together, these works constitute a collection no less substantive than Kingdon-Ward's boxes of dried rhododendrons. They are an unobtrusive way of taking ownership of the landscape and turning it into a kind of exotic specimen.

While in Tunis, Johnston dabbled in journalism, which gave him the opportunity to describe the political as well as the geographical scene. All the great powers in Europe—Britain, France, Belgium, Germany, Portugal, Turkey—had outposts on the African coastland at that time, and all were poised to race and grab as much of the interior as they could. The "Scramble for Africa" was about to begin, and Johnston saw, in a moment of insight, that he was destined to play a part in it. "I said to myself: why, if you take such an interest in Empire, do you not yourself become an active agent for its extension? I resolved that I would, and the whole tenor of my life has been changed by the resolution taken that morning under the Moorish arcades of Tunis."

How he was to achieve this ambition was not clear—even to Johnston himself. He came home from Tunis and busied himself with his paints and his pen. Then, out of the blue, a wonderful opportunity presented itself: he was invited by the Earl of Mayo to accompany him on an expedition to the Congo and Angola. Johnston accepted at once and spent the following months reading up on West Africa.

It was also at this time that he conceived another of the great passions of his life: the study of the tangled branches of the Bantu family of languages. There were hundreds of them, every one different, and each one spoken by a distinct tribe or people, but ultimately all related in some way. On this latest trip, and during the many subsequent years he spent in Africa, it was part of Johnston's life's work to collect, compare and classify the various Bantu vocabularies by interviewing

Henry Morton Stanley discovered Livingstone, and in a sense he discovered Johnston too. He helped Johnston establish himself, allowing the younger man to pursue a vision of an African commonwealth that was not so very different from Livingstone's own.

and observing native speakers. He became a lifelong word-catcher, a lepidopterist of language, and his contribution to African philology remains immense.

Johnston travelled with Mayo for some months through Angola, then, growing in confidence, struck out alone to explore the River Congo. It was here that Johnston encountered Henry Stanley. The man who found Livingstone was no longer a scoop-hungry newspaperman; he was by now a kind of African viceroy, working for the Belgian king and known to the natives by the respectful title of *bula matari*, "the breaker of rocks". He became, for a while, the younger man's friend and protector—Johnston always had the knack of ingratiating himself with older and wiser men.

Johnston returned from this trip a made man. Like Livingstone before him, he wrote a colourful book and was courted by the mandarins at the Foreign Office. His pictures were printed in newspapers, and he was invited to address the Royal Geographical Society. At this formal lecture he shared the platform with Ferdinand de Lesseps, the diplomat who was the driving force behind the construction of the Suez Canal. After listening to the diminutive Johnston make his speech in his reedy little voice, the Frenchman remarked: "*Quel pays, où même les petits enfants sont des explorateurs!*"—"What a country, where even the little children are explorers!" Johnston was 26 years old at the time.

The attention that Johnston gained as a result of the Congo venture led to his next undertaking. He was invited to lead an expedition to Mount Kilimanjaro in East Africa. The trip was sponsored by the British government and by the Royal Geographical Society, so the job was both political and scientific. Politically, Johnston's role was to stake out the mountain, to grab it for Britain and so prevent the French or Germans from laying claim to its cool, mosquito-free uplands. On the scientific side, Johnston's brief was to botanize, birdwatch and catalog Kilimanjaro's rich microclimate.

These South African tribesmen have been photographed at the task of making a 'kaross'. This was a sleeveless cloak made of the hide of an animal such as a leopard.

Johnston took several pictures of this little boy (opposite page). The portrait is a study of shyness and it gives no clue of the subject's identity. The boy was in fact the King of Uganda.

Johnston's sense of fun is evident in this photograph of a boy riding a baby elephant (opposite page). It makes a strange contrast with the sombre image of the boy-king of Uganda (on page 179).

This photograph, taken by Harry Johnston in 1900, shows Masai morani (young warriors) performing the so-called "jumping dance", in which they spring into the air from a standing position to demonstrate their physical agility.

As an ethnographer, Johnston was eternally curious about the everyday customs of African peoples. Here he has carefully recorded the technique whereby Masai women wind wire round their limbs for decoration.

Johannesburg, founded as a collection of tents and shacks in 1886, was a bustling brick-built Victorian town (opposite page) by the time that Johnston photographed it at the turn of the century.

Johnston arrived at the mountain in the summer of 1885, and found himself in an African paradise. He wrote a letter to the secretary of the Royal Geographical Society in which he set out his happy first impressions. "For nearly a week now I have been camped on one of the loveliest sites in the wide world. Above me towers in the unfathomable blue the snowy head of Kibo, around me are the green hills and forested ravines in whose profound depths great cascades of water leap from rock to rock and splash the fronds of lusty ferns. Before me lies spread out a vast blue plain, and my vision southwards is only bounded by the rotundity of the earth."

Over the next year, the expedition identified six new species of bird, a previously unknown monkey, a river crab and various insects. Of the 600 species of plant that were brought back, many had never been seen before by the experts at Kew. Johnston also found time to collect sample vocabularies and write basic grammars of three separate African languages. At the same time, he worked hard on his political mission. He realized that Britain would not be able to have the whole of East Africa to herself, and he began to pen beautiful maps of Africa depicting spheres of European influence as he believed they should be. He included his draughtsmanship in his political despatches to London. These maps, which evolved and changed along with Johnston's colonial vision, represent a kind of taxonomy of the African continent. No less than Johnston's vocabularies and the collations of flora and fauna, they are an outworking of the collector-explorer's instinct to label things, to impose order, to classify and to put each constituent part in its proper place.

Johnston spent most of the rest of his life trying to turn his wishful cartography into political reality. Like many explorers before and after him, he put his knowledge of the area at the service of the government and became a British consul. He negotiated spheres of influence with the Portuguese; he became the friend and adviser of Prime Minister Lord Salisbury; he worked and quarrelled with the empire-builder Cecil Rhodes; and he contributed to the imperial business of carving new states out of the great expanses of East Africa.

But Johnston never ceased to explore. In 1900, during his last year in Africa, he proved the existence of a legendary zebra-like animal. It was the okapi: not a zebra at all, but a striped relative of the giraffe. It was recognized as an entirely new genus and given the Latin name *Okapia johnstoni*.

Even in retirement Johnston made one last contribution both to science and to politics. He was invited by President Theodore Roosevelt to come to America and study the conditions of African Americans. Johnston, as ever, went to the task with gusto: he travelled widely in the southern states and in the West Indies, conducted interviews and took hundreds of photographs (having abandoned the brush for the camera). The resulting book, *The Negro in the New World*, was a surprisingly radical piece of work for its time, despite a certain condescension in its tone. Johnston suggested that there was no truth in the accepted and unchallenged view that the American descendants of Africans were naturally inferior to their white fellow countrymen. The observed difference, he said, was entirely sociological. "In surroundings, in culture, in decorum, there was indeed a balance in favour of the negro if you compared his life with the lowest class of recently arrived Irish or Italian immigrants."

Johnston went to the USA and the Caribbean to make an ethnographic study, but he came back with a striking collection of individual portraits. The four men in these images are from different countries, but they share an African heritage and an engaging intensity of expression. The elderly gentleman (top left) is a centenarian from Louisiana; the man in the smock (top right) is described as a "Haitian peasant"; the police officer (bottom left) is a native African, on duty in Durban, South Africa; and the man with the decorated mirror (bottom right) is Jamaican.

Opposite page: Johnston's pictures of the black inhabitants of the USA and the Caribbean have historical as well as ethnographic value. His work was done barely a generation after the end of slavery, and so is a unique record of a society in the process of change.

The same logic, he came to believe, applied to Africa itself. "The continuance of an insulting policy towards them," he wrote of the African peoples, "will join them some day in a vast league against Europe and America, which will set back the millennium and perhaps even ruin humanity." The way forward, in other words, was cooperation. A lifetime spent studying the myriad fascinating differences between things had led Johnston to the conclusion that, underneath it all, we are all the same.

THE END OF EXPLORATION?

Harry Johnston felt that he did not belong to the first rank of explorers. To be a true geographical hero one had to go to places that nobody had ever laid eyes on or set foot in before—and Johnston rarely did that. He once remarked to his mentor Stanley that he saw himself as a jackal, picking over the leavings of lions. And it is true that his time came when the short, great age of African exploration was already at an end.

But it was not just Africa that was giving up its last secrets. Johnston's lifetime overlapped with those of the men and women who would reach the poles, explore the Arabian interior, and stand atop Everest on the roof of the world. After that mountain triumph in 1953, it seemed to many that there was nowhere left to go. In 1980 Lord Hunt, looking back on the Everest expedition that he had led, wrote that: "exploration, in the traditional sense of making major discoveries about the visible land surface of our planet, can no longer be the principle purpose of an expedition."

So, did exploration die in the middle of the 20th century? Have we tramped every hidden nook and cranny on earth? Not quite. To take one example, in 1998 an American team finally managed to penetrate the 5-mile (8-km) stretch of the Tsangpo River left untrod by Frank Kingdon-Ward in 1924. A quarter of a mile past the point where he turned back, they came upon a waterfall more than 100 feet (30.5 m) high. Beyond it, concealed within a gorge so deep and narrow that it was invisible even to satellite surveillance, they found a lush, untamed garden filled with flowers: ferns, subtropical trees, and an abundance of Kingdon-Ward's beloved rhododendrons. If there ever was a Shangri-La or a geographical fact behind the Tibetan myth, then this was it.

Exploration is not dead, but its nature—along with the business of geography itself—has certainly changed. Over the past 30 years the Society has supported 11 major field expeditions, but not one of them has involved giving a sextant to a lone explorer who may have been variously a geographer, diplomat, surveyor, soldier, linguist, botanist, archaeologist, photographer, artist, hunter or spy.

Modern geographers rarely work alone in the field. The programmes run and supported by the Society have consisted of multinational teams of geographers and other experts. Among them were earth scientists (geologists, meteorologists, cartographers), life scientists (marine biologists and ecologists) and social scientists (ethnographers and anthropologists).

These groups of specialists undertake rigorous investigations, often over many years, into the interactions between natural and social worlds. Such projects have concentrated on the study of locations that were known but little understood. They have spanned the arid wilderness of Oman's Wahiba Sands, the dense Amazonian rainforest of Brazil's Maracá, the submarine tableland of the Mascarene Plateau in the Indian Ocean, the teeming savannah of the Mkomazi Game Reserve in Tanzania and the eroded slopes of Nepal's middle hills.

These research projects were conducted in partnership with national governments and local scientific communities. Their results are shared both locally and internationally. This has often resulted

The Mascarene Ridge, a vast ridge in the Western Indian Ocean, was chosen for the most recent RGS-IBG research programme in partnership with the governments of Mauritius and Seychelles. More than 300 people were involved in a varied programme of research, training, education and monitoring activities over a five year period, to help enhance the qualify of life for communities whose livelihoods depend on marine resources. These photographs show the spectacular marine environment and its curious inhabitants
Photos: Paul Kay (below) and Tom Hooper (above)/RGS-IBG Shoals of Capricorn Programme 1998–2001

*Limestone pinnacles in the Gunung
Mulu National Park, Sarawak
now designated a UNESCO
World Heritage site.*
Photo: Nigel Winser/RGS Mulu
(Sarawak) Expedition 1977–1978

in new policies to help protect these distinct environments. In some cases, governments have recognized the importance of these regions by designating them national parks.

Academic geography, meanwhile, has undergone its own transformation. Geographers have turned their attention to the task of understanding more about known places and regions on an environmental and socio-economic level. They have also taken advantage of new tools to help them understand our changing societies and environments, and to investigate the interactions between them. They have moved on from the plan table and compass of old; now they use geographical information systems to make digital models of landscapes. Other technological advances, such as satellite photography and new laboratory techniques, have contributed to a revolution in the way that geographical research is conducted.

Explorers used to take fascinating things away from the areas they visited; now geography's aim is to bring something useful back to those same places. It is a change that the Society has both accommodated and facilitated. At the same time, the Society continues to be an information hub: it gathers in knowledge of the world, then spreads that knowledge as widely and fruitfully as possible for everyone. That is the Society's long tradition; and that is its stated intention for the future.

The Royal Geographical Society ran 11 overseas research programmes between 1978 and 2001. The aims of these programmes are described on page 236. On these pages are some of the striking images of our world that were produced in the course of that work in the field.

The Hunza valley, high in the Karakoram mountains of northern Pakistan, is filled with orchards. Apricots and walnuts grow in abundance, and right, the apricot harvest is laid out on the bare rock to dry in the warmth of the sun.
Photo: Robert Holmes/RGS International Karakoram Project 1980

Part of the aim of the Karakoram expedition was to revisit 15 high-altitude beacons, all more than 2.5 miles (4 km) above sea level. Readings taken before the First World War were re-made—this time with modern satellite equipment, far right. The new, more accurate readings will help future researchers to track tectonic changes in this geologically dynamic region.
Photo: Robert Holmes/RGS International Karakoram Project 1980

In the scrubland of Kenya's Kora Reserve, the termite mounds protrude from the earth like witches' hats. The mounds are quite a feat of engineering: they can be several metres high; they have a "chimney" for ventilation, as well as myriad internal chambers; and they are often as hard as concrete.

Photo: Victoria Southwell/RGS Kora (Kenya) Research Project 1983

Adjoining the "sand sea" of the
Wahiba in Oman is the watery
expanse of the Arabian Gulf.
Bedu fishermen (left) make a living
at the water's edge, some of them
making their catch in the traditional
manner, by casting weighted nets.
Sand shark (below), sardine,
kingfish and barracuda are the
main catch.
Photos: Richard Turpin/RGS Oman
Wahiba Sands Project 1985

The vast uninhabited island of Maracá in Brazil, lies in the stream of the river Uraricoera, a tributary of the Amazon. Its fauna is extraordinarily rich and diverse. During the expedition of 1987, 450 species of birds were observed and 30,000 insect specimens were collected, more than 200 of which were new to science. There was also a detailed study of the island's snake population, of which an "egg-sucker" cribo is shown, above.
Photo: Mark O'Shea, RGS Maracá Rainforest Project 1987

The "rock pavements" of the Wahiba Sands, right, have an oddly fluid and sinuous appearance. This is because they constitute the fossilized remains of river beds that once flowed across the plain, but are now laid bare by the wind. They are, in other words, the desiccated skeletons of dead streams.
Photo: Nigel Winser/RGS Oman Wahiba Sands Project 1985

The sun sets on Maracá. The flora of the island was studied as closely as its fauna. More than 9,000 trees were tagged and measured, and plant samples were collected for herbaria around the world. The work was part of a study of the way in which rainforest recovers and regenerates after it has been damaged by logging.
Photo: Chris Caldicott/RGS Maracá Rainforest Project 1987

The baobab or "bottle tree" is one of the distinctive features of the Kimberley region of Western Australia. The tree takes its name from the shape of its trunk. Some, like the one shown right, resemble slender wine bottles. More mature trees are stouter, like mediaeval flagons.
Photo: Nigel Winser/RGS Kimberley Research Project, Australia 1988

Far right and overleaf, the rainforests, it is often said, are the lungs of the planet. The RGS has run major rainforest research projects in Brazil, Brunei and Sarawak (Malaysia). More than half the world's estimated 10 million species inhabit the tropical rainforests, but many of these plants and animals are careering headlong into extinction before their existence becomes known to science.
Photos: Paul Harris (far right) and Chris Caldicott/RGS Brunei Rainforest Project 1991 (overleaf)

The Mkomazi Game Reserve, right, in northern Tanzania is one of the richest savannahs in Africa. It is known to host more than 450 species of bird, including rare species such as the green-banded sunbird and the white-chested alethe. The reserve provides seasonal refuge for large mammals such as lions and cheetahs, eland, zebra and hartebeest.
Photo: Nigel Winser/RGS Mkomazi Research Programme, Tanzania 1993–1998

The arid lands known as the Badia spread across territory belonging to Jordan, Syria, Saudi Arabia and Iraq. The research project in Jordan looked at the natural resources of the region, and also at the lives of the nomadic herders who live there. Some of these people still live by moving from place to place with their sheep and goats. Problems of overgrazing are being ameliorated by improvements to range management being introduced by the project.

Photo: Chris Caldicott/RGS Jordan Badia Programme 1992–1996

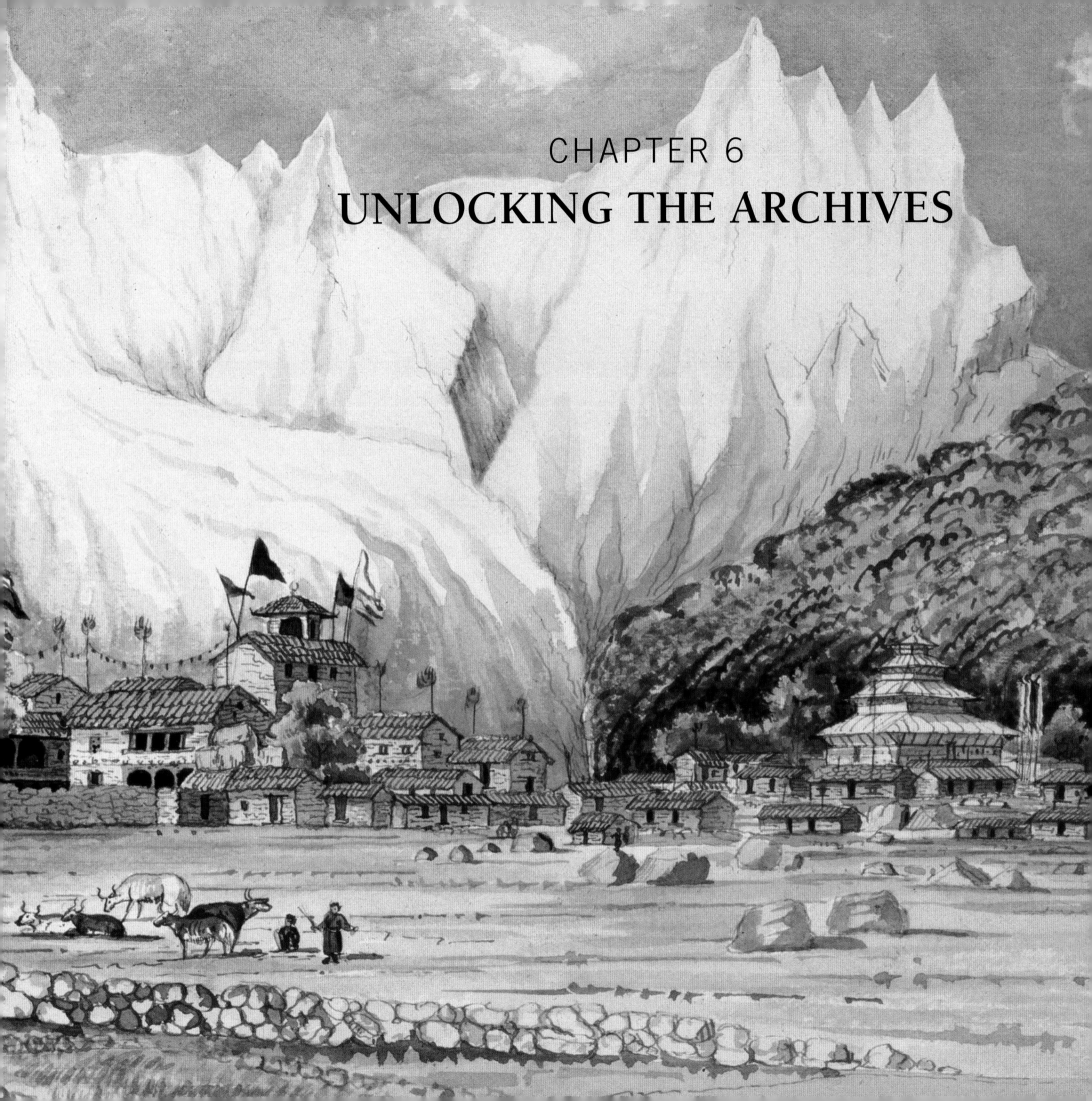

UNLOCKING THE ARCHIVES

Steve Brace, Head of the Collection, RGS

Items in the archive from the 1953 Mount Everest Expedition: Alfred Gregory's picture of Edmund Hillary and Tenzing Norgay at Camp IV after their successful ascent; a diagram showing Hillary's shirt and trouser measurements for the expedition; the open-circuit oxygen cylinders used on Everest.

Previous Page: Henry Oldfield's painting of Keerung, Nepal from 1855.

Captain Robert Scott, the first Englishman to reach the South Pole, once remarked that "it is the duty of an explorer to bring back something more than a bare account of his movements. He must add to the edifice of knowledge those stones which can only be quarried in the regions he visits."

The quarried stones of knowledge have been piling up in the archives of the Society for nearly 200 years. Almost every explorer, traveller and geographer who has ever crossed the threshold of the RGS has contributed something to this man-made mountain of information: some rock-solid scientific research, say, or a precious gem of a personal memoir. It all adds up to a vast and unique collection containing a million maps, half a million photographs, a quarter of a million books, and documents that occupy over half a mile (more than a kilometre) of shelving.

Apart from all this data there are many personal artefacts that tell us something about the people who have made it their business to understand our world. The objects connected with the life of Scott himself are particularly poignant because he did not live to donate them to the Society himself. Everyday things such as the horseshoe that hung in the wardroom of the *Terra Nova*, a mug he drunk from on his last journey, a matchbox that belonged to him, an unused parcel of food from his Antarctic camp—all these gravitated toward the Royal Geographical Society and are now among the treasured holdings of the archive. But no Scott-related object has had a more peculiar journey than a bronze medal that was awarded to him by the RGS after his first, successful Antarctic expedition in 1902.

This memento turned up on a rubbish tip in Camden Town, London, in 1930, and from there made its way back, boomerang-like, to the Society that had originally handed it out.

The relics of other explorers and travellers are no less diverse and priceless: the pocket sextant used by Charles Darwin on his travels, when world-changing ideas were forming in his mind; T. E. Lawrence's Arab headcloth; the shoemaker's measurements for Edmund Hillary's Everest boots, and the tailor's template for Tenzing Norgay's gloves; the Bible that Shackleton left near the wreckage of his ship in Antarctica, and which was salvaged by a pious member of his crew; the tattered blue "consular cap" that David Livingstone raised to the presuming Mr. Stanley on the day they met by Lake Tanganyika, and the trademark pith helmet that Stanley doffed right back; and more sinister, boxes of crudely wrought chains and manacles, confiscated by Livingstone from slave traders in East Africa.

The British Antarctic Expedition 1910–1913 was led by Captain Robert Falcon Scott, top left, as photographed by Herbert Ponting in April 1911; items in the archive inlcude the minature chemical laboratory set, above, carried by Scott during the expedition; left, Dr. Edward Atkinson in the expedition laboratory in September 1911.

The menu card upon which Sir Ernest Shackleton sketched his proposed Antarctic route is held in the RGS archives. Opposite page, the "spectre ship" effect created by photographer Frank Hurley during Shackleton's Imperial Trans-Antarctic Expedition 1914–1917: Hurley used 20 flashlights to create the image during the night of August 27, 1915.

For the first time in its history the Society has now opened its collection to the general public. In 2004, with the help of the Heritage Lottery Fund and other supporters, the RGS launched its "Unlocking the Archives" project. This grand undertaking has ensured that all the archival materials are properly conserved for future generations. It also provided for an extension to the high-Victorian façade of the Society's HQ. In this new part of the building, which nestles in the quiet garden of Lowther Lodge, there is an exhibition space where some of the striking images from the archive can be displayed. There is also the Foyle Reading Room where materials can be studied. Anyone can now come and do geographical research here, in an institution that was once the exclusive preserve of its members and Fellows.

POLES APART

The artefacts in the archive tell an amazing story. For one thing, they dramatize the tension between the pursuit of science and the lust for adventure that lies at the heart of exploration. Take Scott and Shackleton: two men drawn to the same magnetic goal, but poles apart in terms of personality and approach. A contemporary of theirs once said: "For swift and efficient travel, give me Amundsen; for scientific investigation, give me Scott but when you are in a devil of a hole and there seems no way out, get down on your knees and pray for Shackleton." Scott, in other words, saw exploration as the coal-face of science—something you had to do to get the knowledge; but for Shackleton, it was first and foremost a special kind of athletic achievement.

Two artefacts in the archive, one belonging to each man, illustrate this difference. On the one hand there is Scott's miniature chemical laboratory, which he used on his last expedition. Scott's men worked in appalling conditions of polar night and unimaginable cold to gather data about Antarctica's landscape, climate, wildlife and ice conditions. Such was their dedication that they collected 35 pounds of geological samples on the way back from the Pole, which they hauled by sledge across hundreds of miles of ice-fields. So when Scott spoke about quarrying the stones of knowledge he was not being merely whimsical. Lesser men might have dumped the rocks to give themselves a better chance of survival; Scott's men kept them, and the samples were later found with their frozen bodies. Years later, leaf fossils trapped within these rocks provided the first evidence that 250 million years ago Antarctica was part of unified super-continent that geologists call Gondwanaland. Scott, in other words, helped prove the theory of continental drift, although it had not even been dreamed of at the time of his death.

On the other hand there is a map drawn by Shackleton. It is scribbled on the back of a menu card dated March 17, 1914. Turn it over for a moment and you can see that on that evening Sir Ernest enjoyed a dinner of tomato with tapioca, turbot dieppoise, and kirsch sorbet. Turn it back and you have his entire plan for crossing the Antarctic continent. You can see that he intended to achieve this, the last great expedition in his eyes, by striking out from the Weddell Sea, marching straight to the Pole, then carrying on to the Ross Sea on the far side of the landmass. A few strokes of the pen have encapsulated all the dash, bravado and nonchalance of a natural sportsman, and a great leader of men.

The menu map did its job, and Shackleton got the backing he needed for his expedition. But the journey did not work out quite as he had envisioned. Shackleton and his 28 men reached Antarctica, but they never made it to the Pole. Their ship, the *Endurance*, became entrapped in the freezing sea and was soon crushed like a matchbox in a vice. The shipwrecked men camped on the ice for five months, then, during the Antarctic summer, rowed through icy, stormy seas in three open boats to Elephant Island. This uninhabited crag lies at the end of a 1000-mile-long (1600-km) finger of land that points towards the southern tip of Argentina. From Elephant Island, Shackleton and five volunteers again set out on the open sea in one of the boats, and, on the basis of only 5 sextant readings over the course of 17 days, navigated 850 miles (1,370 km) to the island of South Georgia.

But this was not the end of their journey. They landed on the mountainous side of the island, far from the whaling port of Stromness. So Shackleton and two others hammered boat screws through their boots to act as spikes, climbed the mountains with one length of rope and a carpenter's axe, and made their way overland to Stromness. From there, rescue ships were sent back to Elephant Island to pick up the 22 other stranded men. "Not a life lost and we have been through hell," Shackleton later said—and probably no one else in the history of exploration could have pulled it off. One priceless legacy of the expedition is Frank Hurley's set of 120 glass negatives, an astonishing and evocative photographic history of an extraordinary expedition.

WITHOUT DISTINCTION OF RACE OR COLOUR

When Scott and Shackleton ventured into Antarctica's landmass they knew that nobody had been there before them, and that they were not going to be meeting anyone but the penguins. But almost everywhere else in the world, exploration has involved encounters with indigenous people. Some of these encounters were friendly; others less so. European explorers, however well-meaning, took it for granted that they were innately superior to the people whose land they had come to see.

There were honourable exceptions to this assumption, and these are attested to in the archive. The outstanding example is the story of James Chuma and Abdullah Susi, one a woodcutter and the other a freed slave, who in 1874 carried the dead body of David Livingstone from inland Africa to the coast and accompanied it on its long voyage home to Britain. More importantly for geographical science and for the Society's archive, they also gathered up all Livingstone's papers—his vast collection of maps, notes and drawings—and brought them back too. This extraordinary act of homage was, according to the *Illustrated London News*, "a grander and more touching memento of the great missionary explorer than any tomb".

Above, James Chuma sits for a posed portrait by photographers Maull and Co. during his four-month stay in Britain.

The fame of Chuma and Susi preceded them. Even before they arrived in Britain Henry Bartle Frere, president of the RGS, declared that "the Royal Geographical Society will mete out the fair share of praise to every member of the expedition, without distinction of race or colour". Once on British soil Chuma and Susi were invited to the Society and presented with a medal. The president was overflowing with gratitude. "Let us never forget," he said, "what has been done for geography by the faithful band who restore to us all that it was in their power to bring—our lost friend, and who rescued his priceless writings and maps from destruction."

Chuma and Susi stayed in Britain for four months, during which time they were interviewed by the Reverend Horace Waller, who gratefully drew on their knowledge of Livingstone's life and last days in order to edit the explorer's returned papers for publication. They then returned to their homeland of East Africa, where Chuma joined Stanley's expedition to the Nile, and Susi became a caravan leader.

The bronze medals given to Chuma and Susi were coined for the occasion, but just four years after their visit, an Indian explorer was awarded the Society's highest honour, the Founder's Gold Medal. His name was Nain Singh, and he was nominated by Colonel H. Yule, a Fellow of the Society, who said in a letter to the president that "I have a strong opinion that his great merits cannot be fully recognised by anything short of one of the Society's gold medals. Either of his great journeys in Tibet would have brought this reward to any European explorer."

Livingstone is represented in the RGS archives by several of his personal belongings: clockwise from top left: the magnifying glass he used throughout his life; the hypsometric apparatus and thermometer used to take readings for the reports he was required to make for the RGS; a carved section of bark from the mupundu tree near Lake Bangweulu under which his heart was buried in a tin box; a neck iron brought back from Livingstone's 1858–1864 journey to the Zambezi River. He used the chains as props for lectures he gave about the horrors of slavery.

A 19th–century lithograph (right) of Indian Survey porters carrying the equipment needed for the massive task of mapping India in 1855.

Inset: a portrait of Nain Singh who took part in the Great Trigonometrical Survey and explored the Himalayas for the British. He mapped the trade route through Nepal to Tibet, determined for the first time the location and altitude of Lhasa, and mapped a large section of the Tsangpo, the largest Tibetan river.

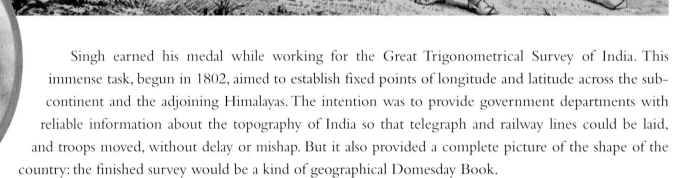

Nain Singh's compass and prayer wheel rest upon the first accurate map of Tsangpo Valley in Tibet, drawn from Singh's survey (right).

Singh earned his medal while working for the Great Trigonometrical Survey of India. This immense task, begun in 1802, aimed to establish fixed points of longitude and latitude across the sub-continent and the adjoining Himalayas. The intention was to provide government departments with reliable information about the topography of India so that telegraph and railway lines could be laid, and troops moved, without delay or mishap. But it also provided a complete picture of the shape of the country: the finished survey would be a kind of geographical Domesday Book.

The project had been pursued for two generations and was far advanced. But in the 1860s the British were prevented from entering the strategically important uplands of Tibet. So they came up with a plan to recruit Indians who could move freely into Tibetan territory. These men were dubbed "pundits", from the Sanskrit for "wise man", because they had insider knowledge of the lie of the land. (This useful term later entered the language in a more general sense: now anyone with an authoritative opinion to share is a pundit.)

Singh was one of the first of these geographical spies. He was trained to take clandestine survey data and to take paces of exactly 33 inches (83 cm). He was also issued a *mala*, a Tibetan rosary, but this one had 100 beads rather than the 108 of Buddhist tradition. By keeping the length of his pace constant and turning a bead every 100 paces, Singh was able to measure out precisely 5 miles (8 km) with each complete circuit of the beads on his rosary. So, dressed as a lama, he entered Tibet and walked along the Upper Brahmaputra, counting every step as he went. All his calculations were noted on strips of paper and concealed inside a prayer wheel. He determined, among other things, the exact geographical position of Lhasa when he went there in 1865.

One account of Singh's journey into Tibet says that he surveyed a stretch of more than 1200 miles (1930 km) of previously unrecorded land. Along the way he made 500 altitude observations by noting the time taken to boil water. An incidental outcome of the survey was that it determined the heights of some of the great peaks in the Himalayas. The highest of them all was named by the British after the officer who had run the survey with great zeal in the 1830s: Colonel George Everest.

BLAZING A TRAIL

If the achievements of indigenous peoples in exploration often went unrecognized by the Society and by society at large, then so did those of another group: the small but important contingent of female explorers and travellers. In 1860 Lady Franklin, the determined widow of the explorer John Franklin, had been recognized for her "self-sacrificing perseverance in sending out expeditions to ascertain the fate of her husband". But Lady Franklin was no explorer—she was rather, through the outworking of her grief, an energetic promoter of exploration.

One of the first women explorers to earn the respect of the RGS was Isabella Bird Bishop. But while she was travelling in the Far East her younger contemporary, Mary Kingsley, was blazing a trail for European womanhood through some of the most inhospitable parts of West Africa. Like Gertrude Bell in Arabia, she made a name for herself by being utterly fearless, and by making it her business to understand the outlook and the psychology of the peoples she lived with and moved among. This made her naturally egalitarian in matters of race, and she derided as absurd the then-common idea that Africans needed to be raised up to European levels of civilization. "A black man is no more an undeveloped white man than a rabbit is an undeveloped hare," she said.

Kingsley applied the same sharp wit and good sense to the question of female explorers. Although she was the first woman to climb to the peak of Mount Cameroon, she preferred to say that she was "the third Englishman" to do so. And for all her deep knowledge of West Africa, she never felt inclined to adopt African ways. She always wore European dress, and objected to the rumour that she wore trousers in Africa (she did, however, carry a monkey on her shoulder during visits to London).

The Royal Geographical Society's archive contains the moleskin hat that Mary Kingsley always wore on her travels, even though she was just the sort of female traveller that many highly placed Fellows within the RGS objected to during her time. The admittance of women to the Society was vehemently resisted until long after Mary Kingsley's death in 1900. At that time the misogynist view was being set out most vocally by Lord Curzon who, on winning a vote against the admission of women, wrote triumphantly: "I have pulled off my combat against the ladies at the RGS successfully … All the papers are very much down on me since women's emancipation is the fashionable tomfoolery of the day." He fuelled the flames by telling *The Times* that "women's sex and training render them unfitted for exploration".

That view was already pretty untenable when Curzon expressed it. So it is ironic that he was the incumbent president of the Society when, in 1913, women were finally admitted on equal terms. And it is doubly ironic that his eldest daughter, Baroness Ravensdale, was in 1959 elected the first female vice-president of the RGS.

Top: Mary Kingsley wore her moleskin hat during her travels in West Africa. It was into this hat that she emptied the contents of an African's purse to find "a human hand, three big toes, four eyes, two ears and other portions of the human frame". Above: a portrait of Mary Kingsley with the dates of her birth and death.

By that time women had more than proved their mettle in the world of geographical exploration. Among the many outstanding female explorers of the 20th century was Freya Stark. She was in the fine tradition of outstanding women writer-explorers that included Bell, Bird and Kingsley. She travelled extensively in the Mediterranean, Middle East and Asia, and earned her living by her pen. She was awarded the Society's gold medal in 1942. She was still travelling in her eighties, trekking by pony through the Himalayas. "To awaken quite alone in a strange town," she wrote, "is one of the pleasantest sensations in the world." In the archive there are many boxes of her photographs, each one mounted on stiff card and captioned in her own neat hand.

A DIALOGUE BETWEEN PAST AND PRESENT

A resource as rich as the archive of the RGS can find many uses. The Society has been delighted by the many scientific and historical ends to which scholars have put the data in its keeping. Scott's observations, for example, are proving useful in the study of climate change. Dr. David Barnes, a marine zoologist from the British Antarctic Survey, recently reviewed the 30 volumes of notes from Scott's expedition and commented that "the great thing about this data is that it comes from a century ago. There have been two big phases of climate warming—one is now and one was between 1910 and 1945. So if we could choose when we would like to have historical data, this is exactly what we'd pick."

Other researchers have looked at 150-year-old charts of the Southern Seas to understand the history of Antarctic ice shelf movement; zoologists have compared old colonial maps of Kenya with contemporary examples to determine the impact of deforestation on primate populations; sociologists have pored over the pay books of Tibetan sherpas in an effort to understand the economic impact of the British Everest expeditions.

The records held by the RGS are proving to be an unexpectedly rich genealogical resource, especially for British citizens whose ancestry lies elsewhere. The Society's maps are a particular help in regions where borders have moved and names have changed. Many Jewish families in Britain, for example, are descended from people who fled persecution in Central and Eastern Europe. "Maps are a tremendous help in genealogy as most families only have a name of a place where their ancestors come from," says George Rigal of the Jewish Genealogical Society, "and the RGS has maps that go back probably further than anywhere else." So, say your family originated in Galicia, which was formerly part of the Austrian Empire and is now divided between Poland and the Ukraine. You could check the name of the village against different maps and pinpoint your roots in the modern landscape.

The Society's maps are also being used to cast light on the family origins of British African-Caribbean peoples. Maps of the Caribbean islands give the names of the plantation owners alongside the location of their villas. Since slave owners routinely endowed their family names on their slaves, this information can be used to pinpoint the plantation where an ancestor worked. The BBC newsreader Moira Stewart, in a TV series on genealogy broadcast in 2004, used this method to trace her family to Dominica and Bermuda.

Freya Stark (1893–1993), above, was awarded the RGS Founder's Medal in 1942. In 1928, at the age of 35, she established her reputation with an audacious journey into the forbidden territory of the Syrian Druze, during which the photograph below was taken.

A map of the UK from Claudius Ptolemy's Geography. *This work was a compilation of what was known about the world's geography in the 2nd century. Originally written in Greek, it was translated into Latin in 1410, and became a standard text for geographers over the next two centuries. Many* editions were printed; this map is taken from the 1486 version printed by Johannes Reger. William Morris was a former owner of the atlas, which is the oldest item in the RGS archive. It still has its original blind-stamped leather boards complete with decorated metal clasps and corners.

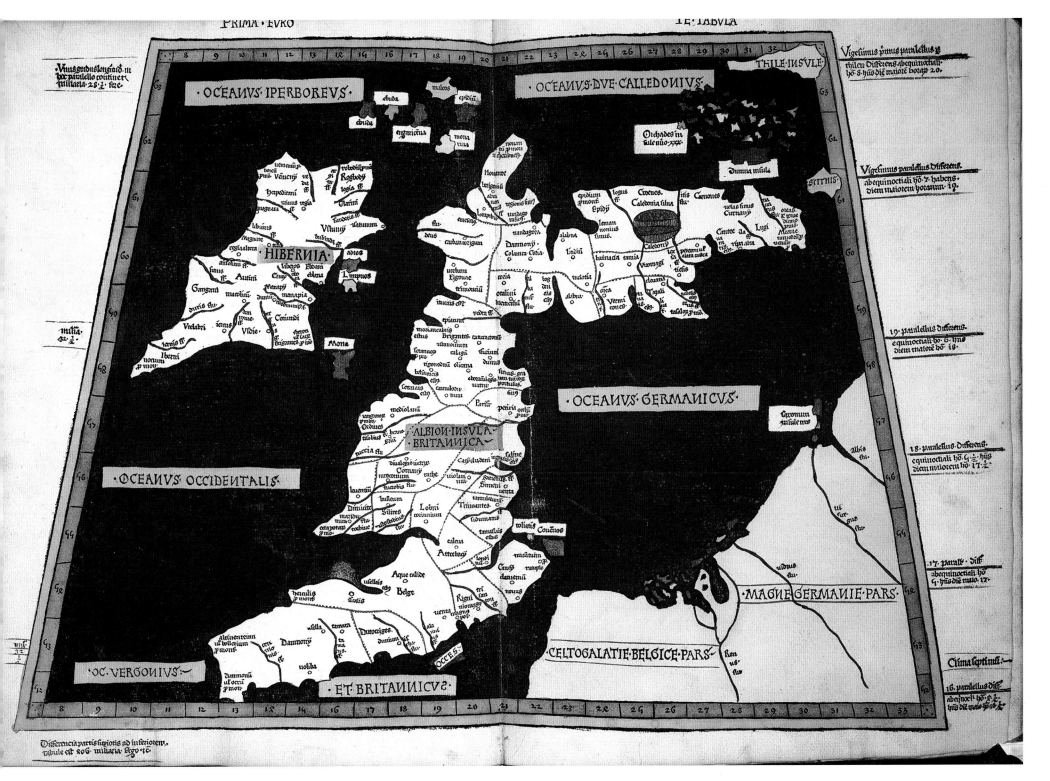

Two examples of Harry Johnston's photography during his 1908–1909 tour of the Caribbean. Above, a Haitian woman with her two children, and, below right, another Haitian offering a bunch of orchids.

It is not just individuals who can uncover the past in this way. Entire communities can take a backward glance at their history. The anthropological photographs taken in the Caribbean by colonial administrator Harry Johnston amount to a documentary record of a bygone way of life. In 2005 the RGS put on an exhibition of many of these pictures and invited elderly African-Caribbean people in London to comment on them. Their insights and memories provided new information about the content of the photographs, and at the same time gave visitors to the exhibition a vision of a world that might easily have vanished and left no trace. The exhibition was, in effect, a dialogue between the past and the present, and between the islands of the Caribbean and the colder island to which some Caribbean people came to live.

Individual histories, community histories and even national histories are contained within the archive. The Society, for example, holds a collection of 229 paintings and drawings made in the 19th century by Henry Oldfield, a British doctor who was working in Nepal. His pictures are the earliest known depictions of the Nepali landscape, its people, and its towns. These images have been used by Nepali scholars as an accurate guide to the original appearance of Nepal's historic buildings. The best illustration of this among Oldfield's work is a drawing of Kathmandu's Bhimsen tower that proves beyond any doubt that the building was wrongly reconstructed after it was damaged by an earthquake in 1934.

The Royal Geographical Society is still collecting material for Scott's "edifice of knowledge". New acquisitions continue to accrue. Among them are maps of the former Soviet Union—cartographical secrets which became available only at the end of the 1990s, some years after the fall of communism. And the digital revolution, combined with satellite technology and computer modelling, has created a whole new category of image—not to say, a whole new way of looking at the planet.

Generations of explorers, geographers and field scientists put themselves through all manner of hardship because they were driven by the desire for knowledge. That same curious instinct is present in each of us, and it explains why the archive of the RGS exists: because this is our world, and we can't help wanting to find out things about it.

The Society holds several paintings by Dr. Oldfield, a surgeon at the British Residency in Kathmandu between 1850–1863. Opposite page, his rendition of the summer house in the Royal Garden in Patan, and, right, part of a writing set he collected while a resident in Nepal.

RESEARCH PROGRAMMES

The Royal Geographical Society has run 11 major multidisciplinary overseas research programmes since 1978. These projects are funded with the assistance of major corporate donors, charitable donations and research grants. The Society works only at the invitation of host governments and in close cooperation with local scientists and educational establishments. The findings from RGS-IBG projects are presented first in the host country, to enable the results to be of benefit to local conservation and development priorities.

MULU (SARAWAK), MALAYSIA (1977–1978)

A study of the newly gazetted Gunung Mulu National Park, Sarawak, to make recommendations for the future management and development of this tropical forest reserve. Over a period of 15 months, 115 scientists carried out 50 separate projects including forest ecology and cave surveys, each of which demonstrated the remarkable diversity of the forest in the park. Mulu became a World Heritage site in 2000.

INTERNATIONAL KARAKORAM PROJECT, PAKISTAN (1980)

An international, interdisciplinary expedition that examined earth science problems in the Karakoram Mountains of northern Pakistan. This expedition, marking the 150th anniversary of the RGS, studied the Karakoram mountains, one of the world's most chaotic and unstable landscapes. It was a testing ground for theories about continental drift, mountain building and decay, and a chance to study the effect of ever-present hazards on the local population: earthquakes, floods, glacier surges, mud-flows and rock-falls.

KORA RESEARCH PROJECT, KENYA (1983)

A detailed ecological inventory of the Kora National Reserve, Kenya, for the Wildlife Conservation and Management Department of the National Government, so it could plan for the future management and utilization of the conservation area. The inventory provided a baseline against which to measure human-induced environmental changes. An important objective was to find commercial uses for acacia resins, as an inducement to persuade local people not to destroy the trees for firewood or grazing.

OMAN WAHIBA SANDS PROJECT (1985–1987)

A geographical investigation to study the early development of the Wahiba Sands (now known as Eastern Sands), its ecosystem and the impact of recent change. The main objectives of the project integrated earth-, life- and human-science disciplines: the sedimentary and geomorphological history of the Sands; sand movement, moisture and vegetation; biological resources and range management; the indigenous communities and their inter-relationships; and oil wealth and local development.

MARACÁ RAINFOREST PROJECT, BRAZIL (1987–1988)

An ecological survey of the riverine island of Maracá, an important tropical forest reserve in Brazilian Amazonia. The project involved more than 200 scientists and scientific technicians, 130 of them from Brazil, working on four related programmes: forest regeneration; soils and hydrology; medical entomology; and land development. The local partners in the project were the Environment Secretariat (SEMA) and the Amazon research institute INPA.

KIMBERLEY RESEARCH PROJECT, AUSTRALIA (1988)

A joint multidisciplinary research project in the Kimberley region of north-western Australia organized by the RGS and the Linnean Society of London, in cooperation with the government of Western Australia. Amid a landscape that is perhaps one of the oldest in the world, the geomorphologists studied the age and climatic history of the area. The life scientists collected field data and studied plant and animal species.

MIDDLE HILLS PROJECT, CENTRAL AND WESTERN NEPAL (1991–1999)

This long-term monitoring programme looked at the sustainable use of land, water and soil resources essential to the future development of managed agricultural land in Nepal's Middle Hill region, an area vulnerable to environmental degradation.

BRUNEI RAINFOREST PROJECT (1991–1992)

A 14-month project, at the invitation of the Universiti Brunei Darussalam to survey the undisturbed lowland primary rainforests of the Batu Apoi Forest Reserve, Temburong District, Brunei Darussalam. The aims were to explore the complex ecology of the environment and to develop the baseline research and teaching facilities for a new field centre.

MKOMAZI ECOLOGICAL RESEARCH PROGRAMME, TANZANIA (1992–1998)

An ecological survey and detailed inventory of the Mkomazi Game Reserve in northern Tanzania, providing baseline data to underpin long-term conservation plans for the area, which is home to species and ecosystems not commonly found elsewhere in East Africa. The project was organised by the RGS in collaboration with the Department of Wildlife, Tanzania.

JORDAN BADIA RESEARCH AND DEVELOPMENT PROGRAMME (1992–1996)

A joint Jordanian-UK research programme run in partnership with Jordan's Higher Council for Science and Technology (HCST) and Durham University to provide decision-makers, in both national government and local households, with the information they require for sustainable management of Jordan's Badia region. In 2005, the Badia Centre, a permanent research and development facility affiliated to HCST, was opened.

SHOALS OF CAPRICORN PROGRAMME, INDIAN OCEAN (1998–2001)

Working with the governments of Mauritius and the Seychelles from a network of field bases, more than 200 scientists from 21 countries studied the marine environment of the Mascarene region of the south-west Indian Ocean. Alongside this research ran a comprehensive training and education programme. These activities are still continuing under the direction of the host nations.

FURTHER READING

CHAPTERS 1 AND 2

Bell, M., Butlin, R. and Heffernan, M. (eds.), *Geography and Imperialism 1820–1940*, Manchester University Press, 1995

Blouet, B. W. (ed.) *Global Geostrategy: Mackinder and the Defence of the West*, Cass, 2005

Blunt, A. *Travel, Gender and Imperialism: Mary Kingsley and West Africa*, Guildford Press, 1994

Bridges, R. C. 'The RGS and the African Exploration Fund', *Geographical Journal*, 129, pp.25–35, 1963

Bridges, R. C. and Hair, P. E. H. (eds.) *Compassing the Vast Globe of the Earth: Studies in the History of the Hakluyt Society, 1846–1996*, Hakluyt Society, 1996

Brown, E. (ed.) *Geography Yesterday and Tomorrow*, Oxford University Press, 1980

Cameron, I. *To the Farthest Ends of the Earth: 150 years of World Exploration*, London, 1980

Driver, F. *Geography Militant: Cultures of Exploration and Empire*, Blackwell, 2000

Duncan, J. and Gregory, D. (eds.) *Writes of Passage: Reading Travel Writing*, Routledge, 1999

Fleming, F. *Barrow's Boys: A Stirring Story of Daring, Fortitude and Downright Lunacy*, Granta Books, 1999

Gilbert, D., Matless, D. and Short, B. (eds.) *Geographies of British Modernity*, Blackwell/IBG Book Series, 2003

Gregory, D. *The Colonial Present*, Blackwell, 2004

Johnston, R. and Williams, M (eds.) *A Century of British Geography*, Oxford University Press for the British Academy, 2003

Keay, J. (ed.) *The Royal Geographical Society History of World Exploration* Hamlyn, 1991

Livingstone, D. N. *The Geographical Tradition*, Blackwell, 1992

Livingstone, D. N. *Putting Science in its Place,* Chicago University Press, 2003

Livingstone, D. N. 'British Geography, 1500–1900: An Imprecise Review', in R. Johnston and M. Williams (eds.), *A Century of British Geography*, pp.11–44, Oxford University Press for the British Academy, 2003

McEwan, C. *Geography, Gender and Empire: Victorian Women Travellers in West Africa*, Ashgate, 2000

Markham, C. *The Fifty Years Work of the Royal Geographical Society*, John Murray, 1881

Marshall-Cornwall, J. *History of the Geographical Club*, privately printed, London, 1976

Mill, H. R. *The Record of the Royal Geographical Society, 1830–1930*, Royal Geographical Society, 1930

Phillips, R. *Mapping Men and Empire: A Geography of Adventure*, Routledge, 1997

Ploszajska, T. *Geographical Education, Empire and Citizenship: Geographical Teaching and Learning in English Schools*, RGS-IBG Historical Geography Research Group, 1999

Riffenburgh, B. *The Myth of the Explorer: The Press, Sensationalism and Geographical Discovery*, Oxford University Press, 1994

Ryan, J. R. *Picturing Empire: Photography and the Visualization of the British Empire*, Reaktion Books, 1997

Said, E. *Orientalism: Western Conceptions of the Orient*, Routledge and Kegan Paul, 1978

Spufford, F. *I May Be Some Time: Ice and the English Imagination*, Faber and Faber, 1996

Stafford, R. A. *Scientist of Empire: Sir Roderick Murchison, Scientific Exploration and Victorian Imperialism*, Cambridge University Press, 1989

Stafford, R. A. 'Scientific Exploration and Empire', in A. Porter (ed.) *The Oxford History of the British Empire, Vol. III, The Nineteenth Century*, pp.294–319, Oxford University Press, 1999

Steel, R. W. *The Institute of British Geographers: The First Fifty Years*, IBG, 1984

Steel, R. W. (ed.), *British Geography 1918–1945*, Cambridge University Press, 1987

Stoddart, D. R. *On Geography and its History*, Blackwell, 1986

CHAPTER 3

Barr, P. *A Curious Life for a Lady: The Story of Isabella Bird*, Macmillan, 1990

Bird, I. *Letter to Henrietta*, London, 2002

Fleming, P. *Bayonets to Lhasa*, Oxford University Press, 1961

Livingstone, D. *Letters and documents*, 1990

MacKenzie, J. M. (ed.) *David Livingstone and the Victorian Encounter with Africa*, National Portrait Gallery, 1996

Martelli, G. *Livingstone's River: A History of the Zambezi Expedition*, Chatto and Windus, 1990

Schapera, I. (ed.) *Livingstone's African Journal*, Chatto and Windus, 1963

Seaver, G. *Francis Younghusband: Explorer and Mystic*, John Murray, 1952

Seaver, G. *David Livingstone: His Life and Letters*, Lutterworth Press, 1957

Younghusband, F. *The Epic of Mount Everest*, Arnold, 1947

CHAPTER 4

Bell, G. *The Desert and the Sown*, Heinemann, 1907

Monroe, E. *Philby of Arabia*, Faber, 1973

Philby, Harry St John. *Arabian Days: An Autobiography*, Hale, 1948

Wallach, J. and Talese, N.A. *Desert Queen: The Extraordinary Life of Gertrude Bell*, Doubleday. 1996

Winstone, H. V. F. *Captain Shakespear: A Portrait*, Cape, 1976

Winstone, H. V. F. *Gertrude Bell*, Cape, 1978

CHAPTER 5

Burnett, J., Kavanagh, J. and Spencer, T. (eds.). *Shoals of Capricorn Marine Science: Training and Education in the Western Indian Ocean, Field Report 1998–2001*, Royal Geographical Society with the Royal Society and the Governments of Seychelles and Mauritius

Coe, M., McWilliam, N., Stone, G. and Packer, M. (eds.) *Mkomazi: The Ecology, Biodiversity and Conservation of a Tanzania Savanna*, Royal Geographical Society (with IBG), 1999

Coe, M.; Collins, N. M., (eds.) *Kora: An Ecological Inventory of the Kora National Reserve*, Kenya, Royal Geographical Society, 1986

Coe, M. *Islands in the Bush: A Natural History of the Kora National Reserve*, Kenya, George Philip and Son, 1985

Cranbrook, The Earl of ; Edwards, David S. *Belalong: A Tropical Rainforest.* Sun Tree Publishing, Singapore. 1994

Dutton, R. W.; Clarke, J. I.; Battikhi, A. M. (eds.) *Arid Land Resources & Their Management: Jordan's Desert Margin*, Kegan Paul International, 1988

Dutton, R. W. (ed.) 'The Scientific Results of The Royal Geographical Society's Oman Wahiba Sands Project,

1985–1987', Special Report No. 3, *Journal of Oman Studies*, 1998

Eavis, A. J. (ed.), *Caves of Mulu '80. The Limestone Caves of the Gunung Mulu National Park*, Sarawak, Royal Geographical Society, 1981

Edwards, D. S.; Booth, W. E. and Choy, S. C., 'Tropical Rainforest Research – Current Issues, Proceedings of the Conference held in Bandar Seri Begawan, April 1993', *Monographiae Biologicae*, Vol. 74, Kluwer Academic Publishers, 1996

Furley, Peter A. (ed.) *The Forest Frontier: Settlement and Change in Brazilian Roraima*, Routledge, 1994

Gardner, R. and Jenkins, A. *Land Use, Soil Conservation and Water Resource Management in the Nepal Middle Hills*. Final Report for the Department for International Development, London. 'A joint research programme by the Soil Science Division, Kathmandu; Institute of Hydrology and Royal Geographical Society', 1995

Goudie, A .S. and Sands, M. J. S., 'The Kimberley Research Project, Western Australia 1988, A Report,' *Geographical Journal*, Vol. 155, pp. 161–166, 1989

Hanbury-Tenison, A.R., (1980) *Mulu: The Rain Forest*, Weidenfeld and Nicolson, 1980

Hemming, John H. Ratter and James, A., *Maracá - Rainforest Island*, Macmillan, 1993

Hemming, John H. (ed.) *The Rainforest Edge. Plant and Soil Ecology of Maracá Island, Brazil,* Manchester University Press, 1994

Jermy, A. Clive and Kavanagh, Kathryn P. (eds.), 'Gunung Mulu National Park, Sarawak: An Account of its Environment and Biota being the Results of the Royal Geographical Society/Sarawak Government Expedition and Survey l977–l978', *Sarawak Museum Journal*, Kuching, Vol. XXX, No. 51 (new series), July 1984, Special Issue 2, part II, 1994

Johnston, H. H. *British Central Africa*, Methuen and Co, 1897

Kingdon-Ward, F. *The Riddle of the Tsangpo Gorges*, Arnold, 1926

Lyte, C. *Frank Kingdon-Ward: The Last of the Great Plant Hunters*, Murray, 1989

Miller, K. J., *Continents in Collision: The International Karakoram Project*, foreword

PICTURE ACKNOWLEDGEMENTS

Permission to use images by the following photographers has been obtained by the Royal Geographical Society Picture Library:
Adrian Arbib 110; Chris Bradley 78, 83, 88, 90, 100; Chris Caldicott jacket flap (back), 2, 13, 98-99, 140-141, 144, 147, 159, 167, 171; David Constantine 104-105, 162-163; Stephen Coyne 117, 160; Joann Crowther jacket flap (front, top), 148, 153; Stuart Crump 180-181; Nick Eakins 108-109, 168-169; Sir Ranulph Fiennes 155; Michael Freeman 89; Brenda Friel 143; Lina Fuller 175; Bruce Herrod front cover, 94, 158, 178; Martha Holmes 51, 112, 161, 170, 172; John R. Jones 101, 150; Eric Lawrie 76, 82, 115, 173; Julia Ling 95; Robert Maletta 79, 92, 151; Edward Mendell 74, 75; John Miles 93, 96-97; James Morris 8, 11; Steve Razzetti 102-103, 156-157; Sybil Sassoon 91, 166, 177; Patrick Syder 114, 176; Stephen Venables 143; Chris Wright 149.

The following images were taken as part of various RGS research programmes:
Chris Caldicott 212-213, 216-217, 220; Paul Harris 184-185, 215; Robert Holmes 206-207; Tom Hooper 204 (bottom); Paul Kay 204 (top); Michael Keating 5; Victoria Southwell 208; Richard Turpin 209; Nigel Winser 205, 210-211, 214, 218.